On Sham, Vulnerability
and other forms of Self-Destruction

On Sham,
Vulnerability
and other forms
of Self-Destruction

by Jules Henry

VINTAGE BOOKS

A DIVISION OF RANDOM HOUSE

NEW YORK

Chapter 1, 'The Culture of Interpersonal Relations in a Therapeutic Institution
for Emotionally Disturbed Children,' The American Orthopsychiatric
Association, Inc., 1957

Chapter 2, 'Personality and Ageing—with Special Reference to Hospitals for
the Aged Poor,' Meredith Publishing Company, 1966

Chapter 3, 'Space and Power in a Psychiatric Unit,' Charles C. Thomas,
Publisher, 1964

Chapter 4, 'A Theory for an Anthropological Analysis of American Culture,'
Anthropological Quarterly, 1966

Chapter 6, 'Values: Guilt, Suffering, and Consequences,' University of Chicago,
1963

Chapter 7, 'Sham,' University of Northern Iowa, 1967

Chapter 8, 'Forty-Year-Old Jitters in Married Urban Women,' Basic Books,
Inc., 1966

Chapter 10, 'Social and Psychological Preparation for War,' The Institute of
Phenomenological Studies, 1968

Contents

On Sham, Vulnerability
and other forms of Self-Destruction

1. The Culture of Interpersonal Relations in a Therapeutic Institution for Emotionally Disturbed Children[*][1]

All cultures have emotionally toned ideas and beliefs that govern interpersonal relations and man's relation to the rest of his world. In this paper such ideas and beliefs are called *ideo-emotional* (I-E) factors, and I shall discuss them to the degree that they are relevant to the interpersonal culture of the Sonia Shankman Orthogenic School. Formulations such as 'Love thy neighbour as thyself', 'All men are created equal', and 'All girls should be popular' are examples of what we mean by I-E factors. In therapeutic milieux there is often a difference between the I-E factors that animate the *staff* and the therapeutic rationale for the *patients*. For example, the proposition that a patient's acting out should be dealt with as a manifestation of illness, and not as a breach of morality, is a therapeutic

* Reprinted from the *American Journal of Orthopsychiatry*, Vol. XXVII, No. 4, October 1957.

1. This paper is based for the most part on data collected by the author during one year of intensive research at the Sonia Shankman Orthogenic School, and during a second year of constant and interested close contact. The intensive research includes roughly 700 hours of direct observation of interaction between children and counsellors, exhaustive records of staff conferences, several hundred informal chats with personnel, and a continuous anthropological record of daily life in the school. The study was done by the writer on the invitation of Dr Bruno Bettelheim, Director of the School, in line with a grant to the school for that purpose by the United States Public Health Service.

principle; but the proposition that social climbing is good can readily be recognized as an I-E factor that in part governs interpersonal relations of the staff in many therapeutic organizations that meanwhile deny its relevance as a conscious therapeutic principle. On the other hand, when the proposition, the frailties of fellow workers should be accepted as a condition of human living and worked through with them rather than condemned, is an I-E factor for *personnel* in a therapeutic organization, then it becomes impossible to separate that I-E factor from the therapeutic *principle* that acting out by patients is to be accepted and handled but not condemned. In most therapeutic environments it is relatively easy to distinguish between the rationale of therapy and the I-E factors[2] because of the sharp separation between personnel and patients, because of the prohibition on mutual emotional involvement of personnel and patients, and because of the personnel's need to maintain the myth of their own excellent emotional 'health'. If, however, the lives of patients and personnel are drawn closer together, if mutual involvement of personnel and patients becomes central to therapy, and the emotional problems of workers are acknowledged and managed as obvious, glacial realities of contemporary life, then the fading of the distinction between I-E factors and therapeutic rationale follows. This is the situation in the Orthogenic School, and hence the basic propositions of this paper are: 1. No sharp distinction is possible in the school between I-E factors and therapeutic rationale. 2. This is due largely to the social organization of the school.

In order to prove this it will be necessary to give a brief sketch of the social organization of the school. This will be followed by a statement of some of the more important I-E factors, and by illustrations of their emergence in the life of the school.

2. A. Stanton and M. Schwartz in *The Mental Hospital* (New York, 1954) challenge the validity of bringing I-E factors and therapeutic rationale together.

The Social Organization of the School

The formal structure of the school belongs to the type called *simple undifferentiated subordination*.[3] The essential features of this type of structure are: 1. One person (director) is responsible for the immediate *direction* of *all* tasks. 2. The therapeutic task (i.e. the patient) is treated as a *unit* and managed by one person (the child-care worker, called 'counsellor'). This type of structure stands in contrast to that of most psychiatric hospitals, where the structure is of the *multiple differentiated type*.[4] In that type there is *more* than one superior, and the patient is not treated as a unit, but he is split up, and responsibility for his parts distributed among several departments and among several different kinds of personnel. For example, psychotherapy is the responsibility of the clinical division through the psychiatrists; residual therapeutic tasks and ward management of the patients are in the hands of the Department of Nursing through the nurses and other ward personnel; recreation is the task of occupational therapy or some other department; residual recreation, like card playing or the endless putting together of jigsaw puzzles, may again be in the hands of ward personnel, and so on. During much if not most of the day no hospital personnel spend time with the patients in the multiple differentiated systems.

In the Orthogenic School there are no therapeutic departments, but all responsibility for rehabilitation is lodged, under the director, in the counsellors,[5] two of whom are in charge of

3. Jules Henry 'Types of Institutional Structure', *Psychiatry*, Vol. XX, 1957, pp. 47–60.

4. ibid. See also Jules Henry, 'The Formal Structure of a Psychiatric Hospital', *Psychiatry*, Vol. XVII, 1954, pp. 139–51.

5. During the course of this research two thirds of the counsellors were in psychotherapy. Since not all counsellors have the necessary experience, some of the forty children are seen by a psychiatric social worker with many years of experience, and others are seen by a therapist in training at the Chicago Psychoanalytic Institute.

each of the six dormitories. After the child comes home at three o'clock in the afternoon from the special elementary or secondary school attached to the dormitory building, he is entirely in the hands of his counsellor until asleep. The counsellor moves through nearly all phases of the child's life with him, all of the child's life at the school is viewed as a possible therapeutic experience,[6] and the child is seen several times a week by one of his counsellors in individual therapy sessions. It must be clear by this time that this is a social structure in which, rather than being subordinated to and dependent on several supervisors or department heads, the way nurses are in most psychiatric hospitals, the counsellor at the Orthogenic School is directly responsible to only one person and has great autonomy in the execution of her task. This occurs because in the Orthogenic School the director, who has sole overall responsibility, has nobody to delegate to except the counsellors, and because the child is treated as a unit and is not parcelled out among therapists, recreationists, and so on. Naturally delegation does not mean renunciation, and hence the director must exercise constant and active supervision of the counsellors. This combination of autonomy in the staff, delegation-without-renunciation, and active and intense supervision, results in *mutual* dependence and support between counsellors and director, with a consequent radical diminution of social distance between them.

Since the counsellors have major responsibility for the rehabilitation of the children, and indeed for almost all aspects of their lives, deep *mutual* involvement of counsellors and children comes as a consequence, and with this massive outlays of time that extend far beyond the four days on dormitory duty. As a result of involvement, feelings of mutual equality are to be expected, and attitudes of submission and dominance recede into the background, though where an experienced counsellor

6. This is described in *Love Is Not Enough* by Bruno Bettelheim (Glencoe, Ill., 1950).

is on duty in the dormitory, there is no doubt as to where decision and control rest. It at once becomes obvious that power of decision and control over *herself*, a control that comes only as a consequence of self-understanding, is the prime requisite of a good counsellor, and this is a basic striving.

Another consequence of the deep mutual involvement of counsellor and child is that most of the counsellor's energies go into the children. The following question must now be answered: given the exacting nature of the counsellor's task, from where does she derive the necessary strength and incentive to carry on? Put another way, the question is: how does a task-oriented organization in our culture fill its positions when the task is more exacting than most of those performed in the culture, and when, at the same time, the pecuniary return is small? The answer to the second question is that the return from the work invested must be greater in *some novel way* than that offered by most other task-oriented organizations in the culture. In the Orthogenic School the return is the feeling of achieving autonomy. The answer to the first question is that the counsellor's energy is derived from her *need* to solve her own problems in working to become an autonomous human being. Thus the reward is high, and of a kind offered by few institutions in our culture; and the energy source is vast – the inner need to solve deep underlying problems in self-striving and self-seeking.

But note the following: *the counsellor's incentive to work parallels the child's struggles towards sanity*, and *ultimate reward for child and counsellor is similar*. Note also that the *autonomy* the counsellor has in *task* performance (because of the great responsibility given her and the great initiative expected) is the expression *in the social system* of what she strives for in the development of her *personality*. It is a striking fact that three years, the average length of stay of children at the school, is also the time it takes a counsellor to gain a feeling of relative assurance in task performance; and that six to seven years, a maximum length of stay for the *children*, is in general the maximum length of stay for *counsellors.* After this time, feeling they have matured adequately in their understanding of the rehabilitation of children and of themselves, counsellors tend to seek positions of greater mone-tary return or, if they are women, they marry. Naturally both men and women counsellors are among those who, after leav-ing the school, marry or seek positions granting larger incomes.

In the school the children are in the centre of therapeutic and *emotional* interest; for the successful counsellor the child remains the focus of her emotional life for a long time. But this central position comes as a consequence, in part, of the proper-ties of the social system itself, and hence the children cannot be left out in an analytical description of it. The children are present, however, not as *objects*, which is what patients are in most psychiatric institutions, but as dynamic parts of the sys-tem, exerting an effect within it at all times: the counsellor's entire position in the school is determined by the nature of her involvement in the children. This is a concrete expression of the general proposition that persons are members of the same social system to the degree that they are involved with one another. This enables us to state, on theoretical grounds, what most observers know, that *in most psychiatric hospitals most of the time patients and personnel are simply not members of the same social system.*

The placing of the *child* within the intense focus of intellectual and emotional interest, and the director's dependence on the personnel, while he is the principal teacher,[7] result in the de-velopment of a small republic or of a large family, depending on the point of view. This family-republic has its own world view, which sets it off consciously from the outer world – from the world outside the school – so that the references to 'people outside' as contrasted to 'us' or 'here', meaning inside the school, are common.

I will now give some illustrations of the functioning of the

7. Some teaching is done by two psychoanalyst consultants. Much mutual instruction takes place between counsellors.

interpersonal culture of the Orthogenic School, in order to show 1. that culture cannot there be divided into I-E factors on the one hand, and therapeutic rationale on the other, but rather constitutes a continuum; and 2. that this condition is in large part a consequence of the social structure of the school.

The Interpersonal Culture

Since mutual involvement of patient and personnel is often enough to project psychiatric workers in the United States out of the institution in which they work, but has become a conscious and effective therapeutic attitude in the Orthogenic School; and since involvement in *one another* is an important element in staff solidarity, it is necessary to give rather extensive attention to the expression of involvement in interviews and chats, and in the day-to-day interchanges in the school. The first illustration is drawn from a talk with Flora, now a teacher in the Orthogenic School's elementary school, but who was a counsellor at the school for four years before that.

7/13/53: Flora said she was a counsellor for four years before she went into teaching. She did not involve herself as much as she might have. She went into teaching because *it required less involvement than counselling*. She came for a summer's job, but stayed on because Harry[8] got to her. She felt he *valued* her. You start by ministering only to physical needs, and this goes on for a long time. Gradually you can do other things ... Flora said *the counsellors took to her* too ... because they did not feel threatened by her ... She felt also that she would have to change if 'I wanted to survive'. I asked ... Why should one wish to survive? and Flora said she began to get something out of it.

It is interesting to start with Flora, not only because she speaks spontaneously about her emotional involvement in the

8. Discussed by B. Bettelheim in 'Harry – A Study in Rehabilitation', *Journal of Abnormal Social Psychology*, Vol. XLIV, pp. 231–65, 1949.

children, but especially because she helps us to understand that some counsellors, even relatively good ones like Flora, may find they must give up counselling because the emotional demands made on them to *give* exceed what they are prepared to *take* from the children. In other words, what I say is that often the American cultural formula, *give in terms of what you get*, must be reversed, and the question asked, *Can you accept emotionally all there is to get?* In connection with Flora's statement we note also how important to her was the mutual involvement of herself and the counsellors.

Leonie, a very successful and experienced counsellor, expressed her feelings differently:

7/16/53: Leonie dropped in to talk. She said that something had happened this morning that made her feel very anxious, and like withdrawing. It was a personal matter . . . that there was 'another person' [not in the school] who had played a part in generating her anxiety, who had to fight a battle without contact with others, who was not as well off as she, who had *staff 'support'*. I mentioned to Leonie that [in the conference] she had not really, in the usual sense of the term, received staff support. She then said she thinks that the support was in that she was able to *give*, especially to the children. . . Leonie said that sometimes it is the very challenge, the determination to make these children see that you *have* something to give that keeps you going.

As Leonie was leaving I delayed her at the door while we discussed briefly a problem raised by her pointing out the vast importance of listening to other people's talk about their experiences with the children. She *used* to hate to sit at these sometimes hours-long sessions, exchanging experiences, because she knew that the other person was not interested in what she had to say, but was just waiting for her to stop so that he could talk. But she came to realize *how important this was in holding the staff together.*

Self-vindication – the need to prove to one's self that one *does* have something of value to give – is thus one of the well-springs of counsellor energy. But the spring does not well, like water, spontaneously from the soil; rather it is in the mutual Self-seeking of counsellor *and* child that *both* can discover *what* there is to give, and *how* it must be given. This was Leonie's discovery about herself and the children. What she also discovered was that it was the same between her and her fellow counsellors: she at first hated to listen to them, but then came to understand that listening to others, as well as having them listen to her, stabilized interpersonal relations. In this sense, there is a parallel between the involvement of counsellor and child and the involvement of the counsellors *in one another*. Meanwhile, let us note that these 'hours-long sessions' were devoted to exchanges about the *children*. Thus it is from the *children* that the impulse towards social solidarity gains much strength. In the same context, that of the relationship between counsellor involvement in the children and counsellor involvement in one another, it is interesting to note that when the observer (J.H.) challenged Leonie's statement that at the recent staff conference she had had staff support, Leonie countered that 'she thinks that the support was in that she was able to give, *especially* to the children'. *The boundary between children and counsellors has become blurred.*

Before closing this uncomfortably brief discussion of involvement, it is well to take a look at what might be called the phenomenon of *psychic immersion* of the counsellor in the child. After a year in the school Ann spoke as follows of her feelings about Rex, a profoundly autistic child, for whom she had principal responsibility.

9/21/53: [Rex had recently been discussed in staff conference on two counts: 1. His having become confused, when Lucy, Ann's co-counsellor, was on duty, by the noise from a sound truck on 55th Street, and gotten out of sight for a few minutes. 2. The meaning of his stereotyped twiddling of pieces of paper before his eyes. This had been hypothesized to be a screen on which he projected the image of a breast.] Ann said to me that she could not work with Rex if she had to believe that he was confused for any reason other than her relationship to him. She said she had the same feeling about the discussion of the screen – that she could not work with Rex if she had to believe that. . .

At midnight that night I was again talking to Ann. I asked her about what she had told me this morning, about seeing herself in Rex. She said it was true. One of the things about herself, for example, is that she always has difficulty in talking, and Rex can't talk; so when she tries to make him talk it is working on something that is also in *her*. She even used to think that Rex *could* talk but *wouldn't*, just like her; that he could talk, but didn't want to. . . In regard to Rex's getting out of sight: this had happened with her too, but it is impossible for her to believe that this can happen for such an impersonal thing as a loud sound. She feels it must be connected with his relationship with her. . .

It has been stated that the source from which the counsellors derive the immense quantities of physical and emotional energy necessary to carry on in this exacting environment is their emotional needs. From the School's practical need for energy and dedication therefore arise a number of related I-E factors: 1. The counsellor shall be Self-seeking – not in the sense of *selfish*, but in the sense of attempting to create a Self that she can live with. 2. In the school the resolution of *staff* emotional problems shall take place. 3. The child shall be the focus of therapy for the *school*, and the principal dynamic in the development of the counsellor. Contrariwise, no counsellor who does not wish to create a new Self, who is unprepared to resolve her own emotional problems, and no one who is unable to take the sick child as a focus for her own development, finds it possible to endure at the school.

These I-E factors are readily perceptible in the previous statements of Flora, Leonie, and Ann. It is interesting at this point to look at the I-E factors as they are spontaneously expressed in a running dispute between a failing counsellor and the staff, as the staff struggles to make her a member of the community:

7/9/53: At lunch table, after dessert, Grace asked when Nancy was going to come on duty as her new co-counsellor. Director (D) lit into her hard, making the point that her reason for wanting a co-counsellor, viz., that she needed more time, was not the issue; the real issue was how much was she doing for the children? . . . Grace acted in an outraged way and gave him back as good as she got. This was one important aspect of the affair: she accused D of being 'unfair', and of being arrogant and trying to read her mind. He said, 'Of course I'm unfair', meaning that in terms of *her* frame of reference he was unfair, but in terms of the needs of the children he was not being unfair . . . He said also that the way she could get most out of this experience for herself would be precisely in this – that she would be unfair to herself in terms of *ordinary* standards, but thus she would have a more rewarding experience than otherwise . . . At one point Grace said she was asking a 'technical' question, and Leonie said, in an annoyed way, that this [asking when Nancy was going to come on] was not a technical question.

I (observer) asked Leonie into my office afterwards to talk about the dispute, and she said that a great deal of the violence that goes on in Grace's dorm is due to the fact that Grace lets the kids act out too much, and thinks of herself merely as a buffer. Things are in bad shape there. *Grace is an isolate* and scarcely talks to the other counsellors. She does not discuss her problems with anybody, so how is she going to get along? The counsellors are hostile to her.

I asked D about the lunch-table incident with Grace . . . He said that when she asks about Nancy what she is really doing is indicating that she wants to hand her problems with the children over to Nancy, and this is self-destructive, for this is exactly what Nancy would like – to be able to take the children away from Grace. Grace is really not giving affection to these children; she is giving everything to Sue [an exceedingly sick schizophrenic child], and Sue cannot give anything in return. She should give affection to Daisy, Mae, and Rhoda, *who can give her something* in return and could really *help her in the management of the dorm* . . . Grace has no contact with other counsellors, and one of D's purposes in attacking Grace was to mobilize the other counsellors to protect her. D says he really likes Grace, she works very hard, but for *him* – she always tries so terribly hard to please *him* . . . but the counsellors should not try to please *him*, but the *children*. That is the only thing that counts. She does not realize that the way she will gain ultimate satisfaction is by pleasing the children. *They sense that she is trying to please him and not them, and they resent it. . .* She needs a number of set-tos such as that of Monday and today before she'll change. But though she resists on the surface 'Why should she give me the pleasure of a victory?' – she changes a little each time. She walked out of the dining-room after the argument in a friendly way, but she didn't have to; he's had counsellors slam the door in his face. He doesn't like it particularly, but he doesn't mind.

The following of particular interest to the analysis of the I-E factors may be noted in this account: 1. Emphasis by D on the emotional satisfactions that the counsellor must be able to derive from work with the children if she is to continue. 2. Emphasis on school standards as against 'ordinary', i.e. outer world standards. 3. The vigour with which the controversy between Grace and D is conducted, in which Grace trades blow for blow with him. This is obviously a function of the autonomous position of the counsellor. Expression of the importance of the idea of autonomy, which involves *lessening the social distance* between counsellor and D, and giving her maximum opportunity to function on her *own initiative*, could be illustrated by many examples, but the following two must suffice. On 7 October 1953 Martha, a counsellor in her fourth year, said to the observer that she

had gone to D after the meeting on Monday and asked him why he attacked the staff [in connection with their resistance to the psychoanalyst]. D said he guessed it was because it was like giving a present to a child and the child thinks nothing of it, or doesn't like it, and you can't tell the child how much it cost, and how much store you set by it. [Meaning how much store he set by the psychoanalyst.] Martha said to him, 'But we are not children', and accused D of concealing his own feelings.

Telling the director off does not occur in the usual psychiatric hospital; not to mention the *outspoken* resistance of the staff to the psychoanalyst, when he first came.

Autonomy consists, however, not alone in lessening social distance between director and worker, but also in placing responsibility for task execution primarily in the hands of the worker. However, to accomplish this the director must make sure that the worker will maintain initiative in task performance, and not continue to lean on him. In simple undifferentiated systems he often has to do this in self-defence, if for no other reason, for there is probably an upper limit to the number of persons with whom a director can confer frequently before he goes to pieces.[9] We have already seen that D attempts to provoke initiative through emphasizing that the counsellor's job is to please the children and not him. Another way of bringing out the spontaneous initiative of the counsellor is mentioned in the following:

11/24/53: D said to me that only if the counsellor does not know what he wants will she be able to bring her spontaneous creativity to bear on the problems that confront her. It is not possible to lay down rules for all counsellors, he said, because each counsellor is so different, and therefore spontaneity would be interfered with.

4. The dynamic role played by the *children.* 5. The involvement of Leonie in the argument. That is to say, her free and intense involvement in a free and intense argument between D and one of his autonomous workers. 6. The fact that the *detachment* of Grace from the other counsellors blocks maximum development of her Self, and her therapeutic involvement in her children. 7. Detachment from the children (handing over responsibility to Nancy) will detach Grace from the basic source of gratification in the school. 8. The eagerness of the inexperienced counsellor to 'steal' the children from her co-counsellors in an

9. V. A. Graicunas, in 'Relationship in Organization', has subjected this problem to mathematical analysis. See H. Gulick and L. Urwick (eds), *Papers on the Science of Administration* (New York, 1937).

effort to gain the children solely for herself. Since this is an expected consequence of the emphasis on involvement, it is handled in the school, as in any well-integrated culture, as a matter of course; not to be condemned or encouraged, but to be dealt with. 9. The emphasis on the importance of the counsellor's capacity to *receive* as well as to give; for it would deprive the *children* of autonomy, dignity, and a chance at emotional health were they not expected to be able to give as well as to receive. 10. The emphasis on making the children a living part of the social organization, through accepting and utilizing their capacities for organization. 11. D's acceptance of Grace's frailties (still after a year), while he still expects her to change. 12. D's recognition of the importance of *counsellor involvement in one another*, and hence his efforts to mobilize them to Grace's defence. 13. His own recognition that his institution cannot be run on the basis of the 'You-are-so-right-Master' syndrome; that if he wants the counsellors to have autonomy he must 'take it as well as dish it out'.

Discussion and Summary

That every institution develops its own culture of interpersonal relations is not a novel discovery. The extent, however, to which such culture is dependent on the formal properties of the social structure has been given little attention,[10] and most of the effort in institutional sociology has gone into the elucidation of informal structure. In this paper on the interpersonal culture of the Sonia Shankman Orthogenic School, I have stressed the formal structure of the school, and attempted to make clear the fact that many of the I-E factors must be understood as expressions of a type of social system which could not function without them. The fundamental ideas of involvement, autonomy, Self-realization and separation between the world of the school and

10. See, for example, D. C. Miller and W. H. Form, *Industrial Sociology* (New York, 1951).

the world outside the school are ideas without which it would be impossible to run an institution having the type of social organization possessed by the school. Of course, I do not say that the social structure *causes* the I-E system, but urge rather the close interdependence of the two. Nor do I argue that the personality of personnel and director are not part and parcel of the process through which the integration of social system and values occurs. Indeed I consider, and have even pointed out, that personalities unsuited to such an environment have to withdraw. It is very important to take note, however, of the fact that there is a tight relationship between I-E factors and formal structure, in the sense that one cannot expect people to follow a system of *I-E factors* unless the formal properties of the *social system* make it possible to do so. Specifically, if one wants workers to be dedicated, autonomous and involved, then the formal structure of the organization must make this possible. So also, if the formal structure precipitates workers into involvement with the patients, it is folly to try to prevent it unless the structure is changed. Finally, if one wants workers to remain *uninvolved*, lacking in autonomy and dedication to the task, and *uninterested* in Self-realization, the formal structure of the contemporary psychiatric hospital is the social device *par excellence* for achieving these goals.[11].

11. I am indebted to Miss Arlene Petersen for assistance in the analysis of the I-E factors.

2. Personality and Ageing – with Special Reference to Hospitals for the Aged Poor[*][1]

I

This paper is based on a study of a large public institution for the chronically sick and aged poor, a cheap private institution for the same kind of patients, and a relatively high-priced hospital for those who are sick and aged but financially well off (not discussed here). The purpose of the study was to explore the effectiveness of skilled nursing care in restoring personality to hospitalized aged individuals. One group of skilled nurses gave care to the patients, while another group observed the general ongoing life of the hospital round the clock. What I have to say is based on the latter section of the study.

Since a very large proportion of the poor are aged individuals,[2] many of whom will end their days or at least spend a great deal of their terminal time in public institutions or very cheap private ones,[3] it is imperative to understand the nature of the peculiar institutional processes that make these last days, months, or years more miserable than necessary. Largely

* Reprinted from John C. McKinney and Frank T. DeVyver (eds) *Aging and Social Policy* (New York, 1966). This study was supported by National Institute of Health (GN 5535).

1. Study supported by National Institute of Health (GN 5535).

2. See Michael Harrington, *The Other America* (New York, 1962).

3. For comparison of a public institution, a cheap private one, and a more expensive one, see Jules Henry, *Culture against Man* (New York, 1963), Chapter 10.

because of low budgetary allocations per patient, as in the public case, and also because of the necessity of realizing a profit in the private case, such institutions suffer parallel inadequacies. Factual descriptions of such institutions can communicate to an audience their general dehumanizing characteristics, but theoretical analysis of the processes that generate them is also necessary in order to suggest points of entry for ameliorative action and to clarify the social dynamics of institutional inhumanity. Inhumanity is a strong inherent tendency in *Homo sapiens*, and in our culture it achieves its finest flowering among the lower levels of the population, because their inhumanity to one another – a common enough feature of the more refined dimensions of society also – is compounded by the inhumanity of the outer world to which they are especially vulnerable and often by the physical inability of the poor to take care of one another. The world's inhumanity to the aged poor and sick achieves a special form in public institutions; but it may be even worse in private ones run on a shoe string, where the pressure for profit may exacerbate certain features also present in public institutions. This paper concentrates on general theoretical considerations that cover salient issues having to do with organizational dynamics in both types of institutions, taking for a model a public one as representing the less extreme case. The reader will therefore bear in mind that usually what is said of the public institution may be true of certain private ones also, only 'more so'.

2

Sociology and anthropology have a traditional way of thinking about person and personality that derives from Émile Durkheim.[4] In this frame of reference 'the essential element of the

4. *Elementary Forms of the Religious Life*, translated by Joseph Ward Swain (New York, 1947) See especially pp. 269–72.

personality is the social part of us'[5] and a 'person' is the embodiment of 'all which represents society in us'. If one looks in reverse at this idea of 'representation of society in us', it becomes clear that a being in whom society ceases to be represented, in the broadest sense, can no longer be a person. If we view the idea of person from the standpoint of process, that is, of becoming a person, we perceive that all events that relate or bind one to the social system can be called *personalizing*. It follows that everything that detaches him from the social system can be called *depersonalizing*. Thus in the theoretical formulation presented here, depersonalization refers to a social process, not to a psychic state. Meanwhile we are aware that, as Bird[6] has made clear, in psychiatry depersonalization refers 'to . . . neurotic feelings of unreality'. In this paper I do not use depersonalization in that sense.

3

Individuals are persons to the degree that they are attached to the social system – the complex of interpersonal and institutional relations. For example, in our culture legitimacy, the social recognition of the attachment of a child to a family, an essential part of the social system, is acquired by a child born of a legal marriage and symbolized in the birth certificate. However, the marriage of the parents is actually the first jural act that binds children to the social system; the issuance of the birth certificate is the second. The child born out of wedlock is less attached to the social system and, by that token, less a social person than a legitimate child. Attachment of the individual to the social system is thus indicated by processes and/or events which bind him to and make him a member of it. The dependence of this binding on specific social events can be under-

5. ibid, p. 272.
6. Brian Bird, 'Depersonalization', *AMA Archives of Neurology and Psychiatry*, Vol. LXXX, 1958, 467–76.

stood by examining the relationship in some societies between personalization – degree of membership in the society – and age. Common in anthropological reports are statements to the effect that in a given society infants are mourned or missed less than older children and older children less than adults. The failure of some societies to be deeply moved by the loss of infants or young children is structurally related to the fact that the latter make little or no contribution to the economy, but also to the circumstance that in such societies they have not passed through the ceremonials which attach them to the socio-religious system.

Personalization is measurable by the number and importance of the processes an individual has gone through, and the socially significant symbols – a name, circumcision, taboos – he has acquired. Among the Murngin of Australia[7] the boy moves through a series of initiation rites, each one of which makes him more and more a Murngin. In our society a middle-class child begins life with the acquisition of legitimate parents, a name, identification tag, blanket, crib, and bottle. He moves on to spoon, high chair, and plate – material and ceremonial indicators of social status of children. Personalization of the child also involves acquisition of sphincter control, proper sleeping and eating habits, succeeding in school, and so on. At each point, as each process is completed and the symbol acquired, the child's position as a personalized being is measurable by what he has acquired and where he stands in the succession of ceremonials. He struggles not so much to master the cultural tasks as to acquire those symbols – 'a child who does not wet', 'a child who goes to school', 'a man with a job' – which tie him to the social structure and compel people to recognize him as a person.

It can be seen from the above that personalization involves not only the acquisition of certain symbols and statuses, but also, in our culture, a series of successes. By that token a person

7. See W. Lloyd Warner, *A Black Civilization* (New York, 1937).

who fails or who has lost the capacity to succeed is less a person, because he has withdrawn from the success mechanism. Thus, just as the child who still 'has accidents' is not as much a person as the one who has mastered his sphincters, so the old person who becomes incontinent loses the right to personality. Children who fail in school may never become people at all; this is the experience of masses of slum children. For such failure the culture destroys them by deprivation of income. Since old people in our culture who have withdrawn or have been displaced from the occupational system can no longer succeed or fail, they are scarcely people at all – unless, of course, they can still symbolize their past success by continued consumption capability. In this way retention of consumption capability, even after having withdrawn from the success machinery, is taken as adequate *quid pro quo* for success, because through it an indispensable service is rendered to the economy.

The acquisition of certain symbols and successes compels society to recognize personality; thus such acquisition exerts a moral force, even though existence of the latter may never be codified.[8] Similarly, the absence of the symbols and successes deprives one of moral force. A child who cannot control his sphincters cannot compel people to treat him as if he could, if for no other reason than that they are afraid of getting dirty. Anyone who puts people in danger of getting dirty loses personality. Yet something else is involved in the attainment and retention of sphincter control: it is a primordial demonstration of self-control and self-mastery. *Mutatis mutandis*, loss of sphincter control in old age may dirty other people, and it demonstrates loss of self-control. A person who has failed or who has withdrawn from the success mechanism loses most of his moral

8. Only when this is understood can the legend of Esau be understood by a modern; for Esau, having sold his birthright, had detached himself from the social system and ceased thereby to be a person. Having committed this enormous crime against himself, Jacob's businesslike swindling of Esau pales into insignificance.

force in the society. Even though he retains consumption capability it is difficult for people to listen to him, for he has lost the inherent moral force that accrues to one who still fights within the success system. Thus all who are still warriors in the war of success and failure are by that token more endowed with moral force than those who are not. Culture awards personality to those who fight its symbolic battles. Hence a child who is not yet in the economic system is less a person than the adolescent who is fighting.

Several factors make it clear that utilitarian notions such as survival or productivity have nothing to do with the moral force deriving from activity within the economic system. The first comes from those tribal cultures like Alor,[9] Kwakiutl,[10] and Trobriands[11] where there is a sharp division between the economics of prestige and the economics of essential production. In these cultures the honorific economic system has nothing to do with the essentials of life or mere biological survival, for it is occupied with the manipulation of largely inessential objects; it is expertise in, and initiation into, such manipulation that confers personality. On the other hand, if a man in these cultures does well at the economics of essential production only, he has no social personality. Furthermore the women, though excellent at the production of essentials, are largely without honour. In our culture disdain for the old has less to do with their withdrawal from the economic system as a productive system than with their leaving the economic system that serves as an engine for generating personality.

The second set of factors derives from the realm of the voluntary work that is done without compensation by middle-class housewives in our culture. Many women find little satisfaction in such work because it is done without compensation. It is

9. Cora Dubois, *The People of Alor* (Minneapolis, 1944).

10. Ruth Benedict, *Patterns of Culture* (Boston, 1934).

11. Bronislaw Malinowski, *Argonauts of the Western Pacific* (New York, 1922).

clear that what is missing in voluntary work is its lack of connection with the personality-conferring mechanism; any compensated job, regardless of how inessential it is, is more valued by such women than voluntary work, even though the latter is essential.[12]

In all cultures the nature of the attachment of an individual to the social system varies through time and is usually related to the economic and symbolic contributions made by him to the culture. Everywhere deference, access to goods and services, the ability to influence social decisions, the capacity 'to be missed', and the right to control the disposition of one's own person emerge as criteria of 'attachment' and hence of personalization. In the history of Western culture slaves have been the most depersonalized human beings, in the sense intended here, and close on their heels have come women and children.

4

When we look at the position of the aged in different cultures from the standpoint of their economic and symbolic contributions to culture and from the standpoint of the criteria of attachment, we see a variegated picture. In contemporary village India the aged man makes little contribution to the economy; yet since he is closer to the supernatural than the young man, and is therefore symbolically more important than the latter, he receives more deference than younger men and still has important influence on public decisions.[13] The same is true in most Australian tribes[14] and in traditional China.[15] It is likely that in these cultures it is the close relationship of the ageing man to the supernatural that tips the balance of life in his

12. In this connection see Betty Friedan, *The Feminine Mystique* (New York, 1963).

13. S. C. Dube, *Indian Village* (London, 1955).

14. Warner, op. cit.

15. Martin Yang, *A Chinese Village* (New York, 1945).

favour, for it is a common, though not universal, experience of the aged in cultures where they have no supernatural symbols attached to them to be neglected to the point where they are starved, treated with contempt, and even asked to commit suicide. Eskimo,[16] Siriono,[17] and Pilaga[18] are examples of cultures where contributions are made largely through techniques of physical survival – economic or military – and where, therefore, the ageing person tends to decline rapidly into a 'he won't be missed' condition.

Yet these functions cannot be considered apart from the concept of *centredness*. The idea of centredness derives from the answer to the question, 'In any organization, whose interests are paramount?' Thus in the traditional public institution for the mentally ill, the staff's interests are paramount; in the contemporary university, the professors' interests are paramount and the students are merely a necessary condition for the staff's paramountcy. In Asiatic families the parents' interests were paramount – and in large areas of India still are – while in the contemporary United States the children's interests are paramount, and no parent who wants to retain respect in the community dare say, 'I come first.' Parent-centredness or parent paramountcy, however, was the rule in traditional China and India for many centuries; along with it went extreme solicitude for the aged. In these circumstances the supernatural powers of the aged were a functional reinforcement of parent paramountcy. Neglect of the aged in contemporary American culture is thus basically caused by the disappearance of the tradition of parent-centredness from Western culture. Eskimo, Siriono, and Pilaga, on the other hand, are not centred at all, in the sense examined here, but are highly individualistic cultures,

16. Mead, op. cit., pp. 72 and 84 (Case 13).

17. Allan R. Holberg, *Nomads of the Long Bow*, Institute of Social Anthropology, Publication No. 10 (Washington, 1950).

18. Jules Henry, 'Anthropology and Psychosomatics', *Psychosomatic Medicine*, Vol. XI, 1949, pp. 16–22.

where cooperative links are minimal. Thus extremely individualistic cultures may lack centredness and also deal harshly
with the aged. The Kaingang Indians of Brazil,[19] a highly
cooperative society, live in about the same economic circumstances as the Siriono; but though they are nomads,
hunting over a territory whose subsistence yield is often
problematic, they carry their aged tenderly about in baby-
carrying bands until the old die.

5

Loss of personality is accompanied by certain changes in social
interaction, some more readily observable in one culture, some
in another. However, all occur in our own culture; all serve to
detach the individual from the social system, and all of them are,
by that token, depersonalizing.

For the purpose of this paper, depersonalization has been
defined as *the process of depriving an individual of the factors that
attach him to his social system*. Where depersonalization occurs, in
this sense, it is related to the declining economic and symbolic
usefulness of the individual – as 'usefulness' is understood in
the particular culture.

6

To the degree that one makes a contribution he will be readily
contained within the social system, and positive social attitudes
will exist towards him. When he ceases to make a contribution
there is a tendency for the social system of which he is a member
to expel him. Figure 1 presents in schematic form the movement of a typical male through a social system during his life
span.

The model indicates that before birth the child is still at the
outer periphery, although he is a member of a social system by
virtue of being in his mother, who is legally married to his

19. Jules Henry, *Jungle People* (New York, 1964).

father.[20] As he grows older he moves towards its centre, where he commands most of the criteria of membership; and as he passes into old age, he declines towards the position of child. In our culture the aged, obsolete adult may readily fall below the status of an unborn, even an unwanted, infant (position 6), but in China and India the individual in late manhood and old age continues to rise in status up to the peculiar, exalted, rather apart position of the aged. At any rate, this is the ideal picture. Extreme old age places him somewhat in the position of the

Figure 1. Model representing the movement of a typical male through his personal community from intrauterine life to death and the hereafter

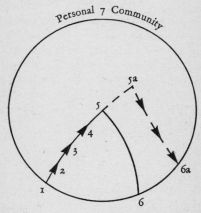

1. Pre-natal period
2. Infancy
3. Childhood
4. Adolescence
5. Manhood
5a. Late manhood and old age in traditional China and India

6. Point of decline to social and material death in our culture
6a. Decline to extreme old age in China and India
7. Posthumous spiritual elevation in China and India

20. In Java the new-born would occupy position 7 on the diagram because he is a god. See Hildred Geertz, *The Javanese Family* (New York, 1961).

demanding (child position 6a). The following from the *Twenty-Four Examples of Filial Piety*[21] illustrate the point.

Tale III: *Deer Milk Served to Parents*

There lived in the time of the Chou dynasty an extremely filial son named Yen-tzu. His father and mother were aged, and each was afflicted with sore eyes. They thirsted for deer milk, and to satisfy their desire Yen-tzu put on a deer skin and went deep into the mountains, planning to mingle with a herd in order to obtain some milk. A party of hunters saw him and were about to shoot, but Yen-tzu told them his whole story and was no longer molested.

Tale V: *Sleeping on Ice to Procure Carp*

In the days of the Chin dynasty lived Wang Hsiang, whose mother died when he was very young. His stepmother, Chu, had no love for him and spoke badly about him to his father. Consequently Wang Hsiang lost his father's affection.

During the winter season, when all was frozen, his stepmother had a desire to eat fresh fish, so Hsiang took off his clothes and slept on the ice, hoping to procure some. Suddenly the ice broke open and a pair of carp leaped out. Hsiang grasped them dutifully and took them home to his stepmother.

Tale VII: *Weeps (Among) Bamboos (and) Sprouts Grow*

In the Kingdom of Wu lived Meng Tsung. His father had died when he was young, and his mother was aged and very sick. During the winter months she longed for soup made of bamboo sprouts, but Tsung found no way to obtain them. Then he went to a grove, where he embraced the bamboos and wept. His filial piety moved Heaven and Earth and all of a sudden the ground burst open and a few sprouts sprang up. Bringing them home, he cooked a soup for his mother; and when she had eaten it she found herself *well*.

21. From Mischa Titiev and Hsing-Chih Tien, 'A Primer of Filial Piety', *Papers of the Michigan Academy of Science, Arts and Letters*, 33 (1947), pp. 261–66.

Tale XIII: *She Suckled her Mother-in-Law without Impatience*

During the time of the T'ang dynasty Lady Ch'ang-sun, great grandmother of Tsui Shan-nan, reached so great an age that she had lost all her teeth. Every day Shan-nan's grandmother, Lady T'ang, would make her toilet carefully, preparatory to entering the front hall, where she would suckle her mother-in-law.[22] By this means the venerable Lady Ch'ang-sun, who was unable to eat solid food, lived in good health for a period of several years. At last, one day she became very sick; and as her old and young relatives gathered about her, Lady Ch'ang-sun said: 'There is no way to repay your kindness, daughter-in-law, and I can only hope that your daughter-in-law will be just as filial and respectful to you as you have been to me.'

In traditional China and India a parent's death places him among the revered ancestors in the realm of the supernatural (position 7), central to the society, yet at the same time at its outermost periphery.

Throughout recorded history, in the Judeo-Christian, Confucian, and Hindu traditions, supernaturalism, parent-centredness, and consideration for the aged have formed one indissoluble complex. Consideration for the aged is readily destroyed by attack on any of these components. Side by side with them has gone economic capability, playing an important, but perhaps not determining role. For example, though in traditional peasant China the father was treated with overt respect until he died, he suffered some decline in status as his economic functions were taken over by the sons.[23]

7^{24}

In our culture poor and aged persons who are unable to take

22. Since in traditional China daughters moved into their husbands' houses on marriage, the incoming daughter-in-law became a female child, subordinate and dutiful to her husband's mother, that is, her mother-in-law and symbolic mother. See Martin Yang, op. cit.

23. See Martin Yang, op. cit.

24. After writing this section, it was pointed out to me that Erving Goffman had dealt with similar considerations in *Asylums* (New York, 1961; Harmondsworth, 1971).

care of themselves have lost the right to personality. From a functional point of view, the institutions to which they are relegated may be looked upon as mechanisms for depersonalization. In this section the process will be examined in detail.

Depersonalization through symbolic means. Here belong those acts which deprive a person of the symbols that represent attachment to the social system. Outstanding among them are its sign systems: communication in general, the personal name, exchange of positive and negative responses by some verbal or non-verbal device. When an individual is being depersonalized in our culture, people do not communicate with him; he is often addressed as 'you' instead of 'Mr Jones' (or 'John'); since little account is taken of his wishes and he is deprived of communication, he does not have the opportunity to give positive or negative responses. In addition, people act as if he were not present; they talk about him in his presence as if he were not there.[25] It is thus apparent that while the sign system is a communications system, in human society – as probably in animal societies also – a more primordial function is to link a member to the social system.

Awareness on the part of others that one's body is part of a sentient human being, and that it is not just a thing, is another factor that contributes to one's sense of being a person. When one's body is rolled around in a bed like a log or merely transferred by hospital employees from one place to another without any indication that the employee is aware of its humanness, the human being enclosed in the body may well feel that he is being treated as an inanimate object. The handling of the body as if it were a thing – as if it were labelled 'log' instead of 'Mr Jones' – is therefore included in the category of 'depersonalization through symbolic means'.

25. This is documented in Chapter 10 of *Culture against Man*, and it is paralleled in a striking way among the Pilaga Indians.

All these processes can be observed in hospitals for the aged poor.

Depersonalization through material means. In every culture, material objects are organized into a system I have called the 'object system',[26] which is a phase of the social system. Objects are organized in terms of 1. assignment to particular persons or groups, 2. certain standards of excellence and 3. use.

Evaluation of an individual's attachment to the social system, and hence of his personalization, must therefore take account of whether he has the objects to which a fully personalized individual is entitled, whether the objects he has are of good quality in conformity with cultural standards, and whether the objects he has are being used for the purpose for which they were intended.

If a hospital patient has no personal accessories such as toilet articles, towels, and comb, if the surroundings are poor, and if, in addition, he is compelled to use material objects for purposes for which they were never intended (washing his face in a bedpan, using a commode for a chair, or a urinal for an emesis basin), then he is being depersonalized through material means.

Distortion in the use of material objects plays a peculiarly destructive role in this environment for two reasons: 1. A large number of the distortions that occur are of a degrading character, inasmuch as they compel the patient to utilize excremental utensils (bedpans, commodes, urinals) for purposes for which they were never intended. In this way a cultural taboo is repeatedly violated. 2. The unconscious confusion between face and buttocks, between mouth and anus, between saliva and urine is well known from the psychoanalytic literature. To the degree that the environment forces these on an individual, therefore, it presents him with an invitation to regression with all its appalling consequences.

26. See Jules Henry, 'A Cross-Cultural Outline of Education', *Current Anthropology*, Vol. I, 1960, pp. 267–305. *Essays on Education*, Harmondsworth, 1971; *Jules Henry on Education*, New York, 1972.

However this may be, what one observes in such environments is the attenuation and even apparent disappearance in some patients of the capacity to experience disgust.

Depersonalization through attack on the shame and disgust functions. There is no culture without shame – the name we give to the feeling that comes upon us when we become exposed to public revilement for having broken a centrally important taboo. The universality of shame and its close relation to culturally central considerations suggest its adaptive significance. Since in our culture the paradigm of the shameful act is exposure of the genitals, it follows that when one is permitted to lie naked where he can be seen by anyone, he is no longer violating the taboo on exposure, because in certain respects he has ceased to be a member of the social system to which most members of the society belong.

However, exposure is merely symbolic of his having ceased to be of adaptive significance to the culture. Much less attention is paid to shame in institutions for the aged poor than in those for the more comfortably fixed, and in our research we never saw an exposed person in the latter, but they did occur in the former. The tendency not to permit shame to the sick and aged poor is simply one aspect of the generally degraded existence they lead. Parallel conditions can be seen in old-fashioned snake pits for the insane, where so-called regressed patients lie about in the cellar, naked and incontinent.

Disgust is the name given to the physical feeling experienced when confronted with foul material objects or foul behaviour. Disgust often though not always, is a spectator complement of the shameful behaviour of another person. The symbol of the disgusting object is faeces; in our culture a paradigm of disgusting behaviour is the public violation of a socially central taboo, such as defecating in public, perhaps. At any rate, it is primarily the disgust function that gets defecation out of the house in human society; and it is the disgust function that makes faeces on the body intolerable. Defecation outside the house – usually quite far from it – and removal of faeces from the body are two abiding characteristics of life in a human social system. A milder form of disgust is generated in our culture by an adult with his face smeared with food. Perhaps it symbolizes regression and is therefore frightening also.

If, then, a bedfast patient is permitted to lie in excreta, to lie naked and exposed to everyone's eyes, to remain with his face covered with food, it must impress on him, and on everyone, the fact that he is not part of the larger social system. Such actions provide the conditions for extreme regression, destroy the capacity to experience shame and disgust, and by that token remove the individual from the larger social system.

Thus the capacity to experience negative sensations is just as important for attachment to the social system as the capacity to experience positive ones, for example, the sensation of prestige. Such considerations can be extended to all disadvantaged classes – Negroes, slaves, serfs, some servants, and so on – for they are often degraded below the capacity to experience shame or disgust. The function of the destruction of the capacity to experience shame and disgust is therefore to dehumanize and to make an individual docile and resigned.

Depersonalization through routinization and deprivation of individuality. In routinization all of certain groups of events in a social system are viewed as identical: all are considered to have the same material characteristics and to be governed by the same temporal sequences. It is the difference between serving each patient food which he selects and at hours chosen by him (non-routine) and serving all patients the same food at the same time (routinization). All hospitals are highly routinized and, even in private pavilions, have relatively little capacity to deal with improbabilities – that is, chance, unusual, special events – in the system.

It is one of the properties of the personalized individual in our culture that he has a right to his improbabilities, that is, to peculiarities that distinguish him from others. In a sense his improbabilities are possessions, inalienable indicators of his self. To the extent that a social system recognizes these, he is a self; the social system, in taking account of his improbabilities, makes a place for him as an individual. In routinization – giving medications, taking temperatures, making beds in assembly-line fashion – a patient is deprived of his improbabilities, reduced to the level of everyone else, and treated like a thing; he is depersonalized.

In a rapidly changing society everyone has, by that fact, a right to his improbabilities; and the contrary push, to conform, is merely a brake on the rush of change. In a hospital for the chronically-ill aged poor, improbability must be eliminated because of the extremely parsimonious conditions under which the institution is conducted and, as has been pointed out, because the patients have lost the right to personality. Thus such institutions may give the impression of timelessness. In their vast reaches time seems suspended; the patients become like figures in a wax museum; it is as if a Piranesi prison, with its atmosphere of hollowness and detachment, had been actualized.

Depersonalization by deprivation of protection. Every social system must provide protection for its members. This is true not only because human beings need protection in order to survive, but because if protection is not provided the reverberations in the unprotected are 'Nobody cares, I am nothing', and depersonalization and loss of the sense of self are stimulated.

In institutions for the aged poor, evidence of lack of protection include absence of control of pilfering, indifference on the part of staff to extremes of temperature (so that, for example, they will permit a ward to become extremely cold while not covering the patients), severe violations of medico-nursing aseptic techniques, and, of course, in the most depraved institutions, lack of food, water, and medical care. While such neglect threatens physical survival, the stress here is on the psychological meaning of such deprivation – the feelings that one is cast away, that one is nothing – and the ensuing dejection and apathy.

Depersonalization through inconstancy and distortion of the human environment. The self emerges in social interaction,[27] and most people require continuous reaffirmation of self through social interaction. Before self-affirmation can begin through social interaction, mutuality has to be established so that self-affirming feedback can occur. This requires constancy of association.[28] However, when there is constant change, the individuals with whom one becomes involved in the ongoing and necessary process of self-affirmation disappear. Since efforts to re-establish the interrupted process probably become increasingly painful, the individual tends to withdraw from social interaction and thus loses attachment to the social system. This is the line of speculation I have followed in attempting to understand what happens as a consequence of constantly shifting patients' beds, in attempting to understand why noisy ones whose beds are often shifted become quiet.

In the situations under discussion, inconstancy arises because patients are frequently moved from one part of the ward to another. As a matter of fact, if staff see patients in vigorous interaction, one of them may be moved. This is a factor responsible for the low interactional rate and for the tomb-like quiet noted.

Just as constancy and continuity of human contact seem necessary to full personalization, so does corporal intactness; if

27. See George Herbert Mead, *Mind, Self and Society* (Chicago, 1934).
28. Experiments have been done on animals deprived of social interaction. It is necessary to do similar experiments with animals whose society is constantly changed, but who, nevertheless, are not actually deprived of associates.

one is surrounded by the blind, the deaf, the dismembered and the incontinent, there is just as great a tendency to withdraw as if these persons were not there. One of the most powerful depersonalizing agencies is the inability to escape from such distorted people.

Depersonalization and staff-centredness. All social systems embody a certain choice with respect to the direction in which energies and sanctions shall be focused. We call our contemporary society child-centred. The cultures of traditional India and China were parent-centred. The concept of centredness implies not only a mobilization of energy towards a group but a possible tendency to sacrifice the well-being of other groups to that of the central group.

Centredness is a culturally determined perception that facilitates the mobilization of energies in favour of one group rather than another. In a hospital in which staff-centredness prevails, the comfort and convenience of the staff tends to overshadow that of the patients, and thus makes a massive contribution to depersonalization. When the patients are poor and aged, that is, have already lost much of their right to membership in the larger social system, staff-centredness is facilitated because no one is bound to centre his attention on those already slipping out of the social system.

Staff-centredness is expressed in a number of ways:

1. *Through routinization.* Routinization of functions occurs when the functions are performed in the simplest and most expeditious way. It means that the employee does not have to think about what he does or take any individual differences in patients into account. Communication is reduced to the minimum necessary to discharge the routinized and highly standardized functions. The emphasis is on smoothness and ease of repetition.

2. *Through the elimination of improbability.* To the extent that staff have to take into account the unpredictabilities of patients,

their task is made more difficult. However, if all patients are calm and quiet, task performance is easier. The most powerful way of eliminating conflicts between patients is by moving them from one part of a ward to another.

3. *Through equalization of functions.* Perhaps the ideal in any task-performing organization is that all roles should be interchangeable, so that everyone can perform everyone else's task. Under such circumstances there is little to fear if an employee is absent or leaves, for anyone can do what he does. Interchangeability of roles can be accomplished by constantly rotating staff through all divisions, with the result that personnel rarely remain permanently on any division. Although this may be good for the performance of routine tasks, it creates an inconstant relationship between staff and patients, and thus contributes to depersonalization.

8

Social-conscience loading (SCL) is the strength of the social feelings of right and wrong that attach to the commission or omission of any act.[29] Some acts can have a higher SCL than others. Thus in our culture murder has a higher SCL than robbery; rape has a higher SCL than seduction. In hospitals cleanliness has a higher SCL than tenderness: a dirty hospital would excite universal anger and probably have its licence revoked, but patients have been treated coldly in clean and efficient hospitals for generations, and the social conscience scarcely twitches.

In the situations of which I speak SCL plays an important role in depersonalization.

Social-conscience loading and task visibility. Since in our culture the social conscience is readily aroused by dirt and disorder in a public institution, major effort falls on the performance of tasks

29. See Émile Durkheim, *The Division of Labor* (New York, 1933).

of highest visibility: keeping the wards neat and clean. Specifically the following are emphasized: unlittered bedside tables; well-made beds; clean floors; uncluttered walls without pictures, calendars, or posters; removal of loose personal property like newspapers and books. Plaques and prizes may be awarded staff teams having the neatest wards.

Social-conscience loading and medical supplies. To the degree that the social conscience can be affected by conditions in a public hospital, it will be more readily aroused by absence of medicines and dressings than by a shortage of washcloths, towels, tissues, or even soap. This is so because the social conscience is more readily aroused by death than by anything else. Furthermore, since guilt and feelings of respectability are important ingredients of the social conscience in our culture, the guilt and sense of offended respectability that follow upon the death even of inadequately medicated paupers readily stimulate society to take punitive action. On the other hand, it seems likely that requests for more washcloths, towels, tissues, and soap might arouse the social conscience against 'pampering' and against 'making a hotel out of a public institution'. Thus in our culture the social conscience is characterized by a polarity which emphasizes survival of the body and burial of the personality.

This being the case, funds are allocated first for materials having the highest SCL, and the amenities and accessories of life (the 'pampering materials') tend to be absent or in short supply.

Social-conscience loading, material culture, and status. In speaking of the object system, I pointed out that material culture is assigned to different groups in line with the status of the group. Thus boomerangs, *churingas*, and bull-roarers are not handled by women among Australian tribes because women have low status. In our culture a person who earns his money operating a drill-press is of lower status than one who operates a book-keeping machine. In a hospital the supplies have the heaviest SCL – medicines, dressings and so on – are handled by the high-status personnel (h.s.p.) – doctors and nurses – and the supplies having little SCL are handled by low-status personnel (l.s.p.) When funds are low, the supplies having the heaviest SCL are usually available, while the others tend to be in short supply. The effect of this is to depress the morale of the l.s.p. and contribute to *their* depersonalization, thus making a double contribution to poor patient care and hence to depersonalization. The shortage of supplies makes it difficult to do a good job of taking care of the patients, and the depressed morale of the l.s.p. contributes to their surliness in dealing with the patients.

Furthermore the effect of short supplies in these materials is cumulative, for it may lead to hoarding, which in turn creates false shortages and throws the staff into collision; this is bound to affect staff–patient relations adversely. Meanwhile it should be borne in mind that since the things the l.s.p. handle have low SCL, l.s.p. can do little to remedy the condition. Thus the quality of patient care, and hence the extent of their depersonalization, is a complex function of the interrelation among supplies, their SCL, and the status of the persons manipulating them. The object system of the hospital is part of a status system, and both are related to the social conscience. The social conscience cares less about what the l.s.p. does with its low-status supplies than it does about what the h.s.p. does with *its* supplies. Meanwhile it is the l.s.p. who are in closest contact with the patients and manipulate the (nearly non-existent) human amenities.

I have spoken previously of disgust and its relation to depersonalization. Here we may note that it is the l.s.p. who are compelled by their tasks to do most violence to their own disgust functions, for it is they who must clean the incontinent, wipe the excreta from the beds and floors, and empty the bed-pans. Thus here, as well as in the object system, the forces of depersonalization operate on the personnel as on the patients. And here, as well as in the object system relations, the tasks of the l.s.p. serve to turn them against the patients, for the patients are the source of the attack on the disgust function of staff personality.

9

A large proportion of the aged are sick and poor and thus likely to spend a good part of their remaining time in public or cheap private institutions. It is necessary therefore to understand the extent to which such institutions may destroy personality, in the sociological sense.

Individuals are persons to the degree that they are attached to a social system, and this involves the acquisition and retention of certain tangible and intangible symbols of attachment. In acquiring these symbols, individuals in all cultures go through certain processes and achieve certain statuses. Taken together these constitute personality, in the social sense, and have a moral force, in the sense that a person, by virtue of having acquired all necessary symbols and statuses necessary to attachment, has the power to compel deference to himself – in short, to be treated like a person. From a genetic point of view, personalization changes through time and varies as the individual acquires or loses symbols and statuses. In line with these considerations, it can be seen that the position of the aged – their degree of attachment to the social system – varies in different cultures.

The process of depersonalization, defined as the process of depriving an individual of the factors that attach him to the social system, has been studied in a very large public and in a large cheap private institution for the chronically ill aged. This deprivation of the individual of the components of attachment to the social system, of the components of social personality, includes depersonalization through symbolic means – essentially the generalized loss of communications possibilities and the negative handling of the body; depersonalization through material means – essentially the deprivation of the material amenities, the generally poor quality of the available material culture, and the use of material objects in a distorted way; depersonalization through extinction or violation of the shame and disgust functions; depersonalization through routinization and deprivation of individuality and protection; depersonalization through inconstancy and distortion of the human environment; and depersonalization through staff-centredness. Finally, since society's interest in its poor, sick, and aged charges does not go beyond material things – including the medical – and the correct performance of tasks of high visibility, humane behaviour by the caretakers is left to chance. Since the caretakers in such institutions are poorly paid, poorly educated, and overworked, they have little incentive to humaneness.

The ultimate consequences of depersonalization are mutual hostility, loss of social capabilities, and apathy.

3. Space and Power on a Psychiatric Unit*

*Reprinted from Albert F. Wessen (ed.), *The Psychiatric Hospital as a Social System* (Springfield, Ill., 1964).

I

One of the innate properties of animals is the tendency to require certain types of spatial distribution when in the free-ranging state. Thus whether they be ants, isolated from one another within their colonial ant hills, robins defending their territories during mating time, or baboons in the African wilderness, animals seem to choose spatial distributions in accordance with innate tendencies. In humans these innate tendencies have been modified to such a degree by culture that every cultural group sets its *own* pattern for the utilization of space. Of humans one can say that they have a peculiar way of perceiving space so that they arrange themselves and the objects they create, or find in the environment, in a manner that suits rather rigid cultural *Anlagen*. One can also say that humans bring to a relatively inert environment culturally determined perceptions of space and then proceed to arrange themselves in it accordingly. We may call this tendency to arrange oneself in space according to certain culturally determined perceptual patterns the *personalization of space*.

At the present time the billions that are being spent on space exploration are an expression of an 'innate' tendency to personalize space. In the particular case the tendency has become assimilated to a power–prestige struggle. This patterned struggle for space itself, a peculiar expression of our culture, is reflected in all dimensions of it, and we shall presently see this struggle operating on a psychiatric ward. Meanwhile we must bear in mind that space struggles also occur in families, where different members are excluded from different rooms at different times, and where indeed the exclusion or the more or less willing withdrawal of a person from a particular room or part of the house may express deep-going anxieties, hostilities, or psycho–pathogenic rigidities. Thus these considerations force upon us the realization that in its spatial arrangements a psychiatric hospital may unwittingly reflect lethal aspects of spatial orientations found in the outer society.

The present paper is an effort to examine the problem of space on a psychiatric ward from several points of view: 1. the relation between hospital architecture and the patient society; 2. the relation between the functioning of the hospital as a therapeutic milieu and the spatial arrangements of the hospital; 3. the relation between the utilization of space and the formation of a patient–staff 'social conspiracy'.

This psychiatric ward was one of two in a large general hospital. The ward contained twenty-nine patients, and was studied intensively, through interview and observation by the writer, for five months. The personnel were observed in interaction with the patients for a total of sixty-five hours extending over twenty-five observation periods ranging in duration from ten minutes to nine and one-fourth hours. The mean observation time was approximately two hours and twelve minutes. The ward studied had an attractive solarium with upholstered chairs, radio, television set, pleasant draperies, and a very large bay window. A short, rather dark corridor that contained wooden chairs and two long, 'hospital-style' wooden tables was situated just outside the solarium, one interior side of which was glass. It was far more pleasant inside the solarium than outside in the corridor. During the first days of the study, it appeared to the writer that there might be a difference between the people who habitually sat outside the solarium and those who spent their time inside. He thus hypothesized a systematic difference between those who sat inside and those who sat outside. Table I gives the results of the study of the patient demography of the solarium.

TABLE I

Analysis of the Ward Patient Population in Terms of Status as 'Insiders' or 'Outsiders' with Respect to the Solarium

Patient	Age	Diagnosis	Number of Times Observed Inside	Outside	Status
Miss O	33	Schizoid reaction	11	5	Insider
Miss T	34	Mixed psychoneurosis; hysteria; depression; cycloid; schizoid	14	3	Insider
Mrs J	25	Conversion hysteria; suicidal	15	4	Insider
Mrs Ac	56	Senile psychosis; depressed; agitated; latent syphillis of the skin	7	2	Insider
Mr Z	46	Involutional psychosis; depressed; paranoid	10	2	Insider
Mr G	62	Senile psychosis with depression	16	7	Insider
Mr I	18	Paranoid schizophrenia	17	2	Insider
Mr H	24	Paranoid schizophrenia	14	2	Insider
Mr C	15	Obsessive; compulsive; depression	10	4	Insider
Mrs U	51	Psychotic depression	10	2	Insider
Mrs F	30?†	Post-partem psychosis	7	3	Insider
Mrs A	30?†	‡ ?	8	3	Insider
Mrs P	23	Addiction	8	2	Insider
Mr Q	59	Involutional melancholia	6	2	Insider
Mrs Ab	60	Psychosis undiagnosed; carcinoma of the breast	12	9	Indeterminate*

Patient	Age	Diagnosis	Number of Times Observed Inside	Outside	Status
Mr Aa	40	Depression with paranoid trends; nerve deafness	6	4	Indeterminate
Miss N	20	Conduct disorder	11	9	Indeterminate
Miss B	39	Paranoid schizophrenia	7	6	Indeterminate
Mrs L	30	Epilepsy, grand mal; psychomotor	7	6	Indeterminate
Mrs K	45	Diabetes mellitus; toxic psychosis	3	11	Outsider
Miss E	10	Psycho-motor epilepsy; speech defect; borderline mentality	3	7	Outsider
Mrs M	47	Involutional psychosis; paranoid ideas; depression	1	12	Outsider
Mrs X	65	Agitated depression	0	10	Outsider
Mrs D	51	Involutional melancholia	6	22	Outsider
Mrs S	53	Involutional psychosis; paranoid type	1	16	Outsider
Mrs V	45	Involutional psychosis; melancholia	0	19	Outsider
Mrs Y	51	Involutional depression	3	6	Outsider
Mrs W	60	Agitated depression	2	7	Outsider
Mrs R	55	Manic-depressive psychosis	0	8	Outsider

* Patients classified 'indeterminate' are those for whom the number in the fourth column is less than twice that in the fifth, or vice versa.

† Age not ascertainable; thirty years is investigator's guess.

‡ Unresponsive, disinterested, uncommunicative.

Observation and analysis of the data derived from study of the movements of the patient population around and into and out of the solarium show that the ward population divided itself into two groups, the 'insiders' and the 'outsiders', fourteen being in the former group and ten in the latter, with five indeterminates. The insider and outsider groups differed from each other in a number of striking characteristics. For example, there were no insiders who spent all of their time in the solarium and there were no insiders who were observed outside the solarium only once. On the other hand, three outsiders were never seen to set foot inside the solarium and two outsiders did it but once. A further indication of the lesser variability in the behaviour of the outsiders vis-à-vis the solarium is that the average number of times the insiders were observed outside the solarium was 3·1 whereas the average number of times the outsiders were observed inside was only 1·9

A striking difference is to be noted in the ages of members of the two groups. The mean age of the insiders is 36·1 years,[1] whereas the mean age of the outsiders is 48·2 years. However, if we remove the two children – Miss E (age 10 years) from the outside group and Mr C (age 15 years) from the inside group – the age difference appears even more striking, for the mean age of the insiders becomes 37·8 years and that of the outsiders 52·4 years. Thus the group inside the solarium – the pleasantest part of the ward, is the younger. This reflects the American antagonism to old age.

The outside population was not only older than the inside, but also more homogeneous. For example, the inside population contained people in all age groups from teens to 60s, but the outside group contained only persons in the age groups from forty to sixty and one child of ten (she appears to have been made 'the child' or perhaps 'the grandchild' of the outsiders). It is also to be noted in this connection that with the exception of this child (Miss E) all of the outsiders were married women in or approaching menopause whereas a considerable number of the insiders were quite young, two being unmarried young women; moreover, six insiders were men. Finally it is to be noted that although the illnesses of the insiders were varied, eight of the ten outsiders were diagnosed as having

1. If Mrs A and Mrs F, whose ages were not definitely known, are excluded, the average age for this group becomes 37·2 years.

psychotic depressions. It will be seen that nothing that happened in the patient society or in patient–staff interaction tended to change the illness pattern of the outsiders. Rather, that the hospital society tended to reinforce and support those lethal interactions of exclusion and withdrawal that contribute to the formation of certain kinds of depressions.

Thus the patient society on this ward had divided itself into two groups: 1. *heterogeneous* – relatively flexible, relatively youthful, mixed ages, mixed civil status (i.e. both single and married), varied personalities; and 2. *homogeneous* – relatively rigid, all women, relatively old, uniform age and civil status, uniform personalities (all but two depressed). The labels 'insider' and 'outsider' thus correspond to two human groups identifiable by specific traits that are all of cultural significance and that all have important status implications in the outer world. Even 'unhappiness', as expressed in chronic depression, is an important negative stigmatum in the outer world, creating impulses in others to withdrawal and flight. We know that in America 'smilers always win and frowners always lose'.

We have seen therefore that the patients divided themselves into two different cultures in terms of the architecture of the ward, which they exploited to their own ends. Of course, the division was not accomplished without some overlap, but it may be that had this arrangement of cultural differentiation been given a chance to age, its outlines would have become clearer; for example, in time, all of the six depressive patients might have been forced out of the solarium.

At this point, we may turn for a few moments to a subsidiary consideration, a proposition implicit in all hospital management, that the hospital shall control the hospital environment, for the good of the patient, of course. An underlying assumption and therapeutic necessity in the operation of any healing institution is that it shall be controlled by the administration and administered benignly in the interest of the patients. When, however, we examine this ward, we discover that although in many respects the hospital did control the environment, the patients to a very considerable and important degree created their own *culture*. It is thus clear that in this respect the hospital was not 'running' the patients: the patients were 'running' the hospital. The patients, by imposing distinctions between youth and age, fertile and infertile, lively and quiet, dragged into the hospital some of the questionable standards of the outer world, using them in a way that could be in the long run, and very likely was in the short run, harmful.

Meanwhile it is very important to note that this patient-created culture was reinforced by the students and attendants. I say 'by the students and attendants' rather than 'by the nurses' because, although there was a very satisfactory number of trained psychiatric nurses relative to the size of the patient population, the nurses had little contact with the patients, devoting themselves largely to charting and domestic tasks. Analysis of patient–employee interaction (See Tables II and III) shows that on the average the insiders were drawn into games – mostly checkers and cards – by the employees four times as often as the outsiders, and that the younger people participated on the average more frquently than the older. Seventy per cent of the outsiders never participated in these games at all, but this was true of only 29 per cent of the insiders.

Thus the employees appear to reinforce and to follow the norms of the patient culture. It appears likely that this was due to the fact that the employees shared the attitude of the patients. There was thus formed a kind of patient–personnel conspiracy to reproduce and reinforce on the ward the mirror image of the culture of the outer world. Since the society created spontaneously by these patients resembled that of the outer world and was reinforced by the hospital personnel, the hypothesis is suggested that the more patient cultures, however contra-therapeutic they may be, resemble those of the outer world, the

TABLE II

Patient Participation in Games with Employees as Related to Patient Status as In- or Outsider

Patient	Age	Status of Patient	Number of Times in Games	Number of Days Observed	Game-Day Ratio
Miss T	34	Insider	5	10	·50
Mr H	24	Insider	5	11	·45
Miss N	20	Indeterminate	6	15	·40
Mrs U	51	Insider	2	6	·33
Mrs P	23	Insider	4	13	·31
Mrs L	30	Indeterminate	2	7	·29
Mr I	18	Insider	2	9	·22
Mrs W	60	Outsider	2	10	·20
Mr C	15	Insider	3	16	·19
Miss O	33	Insider	3	16	·19
Miss E	10	Outsider	1	6	·17
Mrs F	30?	Insider	1	7	·14
Mrs Y	51	Outsider	1	11	·09
Mr Aa	40	Indeterminate	1	14	·07
Miss B	39	Indeterminate	2	28	·07
Mrs Ab	60	Indeterminate	1	15	·07
Mr Z	46	Insider	1	16	·06
Mrs J	25	Insider	1	16	·06
Mrs A	30?	Insider	0	8	0
Mrs D	51	Outsider	0	15	0
Mr G	62	Insider	0	16	0
Mrs K	45	Outsider	0	4	0
Mrs M	47	Outsider	0	6	0
Mr Q	59	Insider	0	6	0
Mrs R	55	Outsider	0	7	0
Mrs S	53	Outsider	0	8	0
Mrs V	45	Outsider	0	9	0
Mrs X	65	Outsider	0	5	0
Mrs Ac	56	Insider	0	13	0

greater is the tendency of the hospital personnel to reinforce
them, provided, of course, that such structures do not run
counter to the personnel's own interests. These data suggest
also that patient social structures, to the extent that they resemble the outer world, have low visibility and hence may pass
unnoticed, with all their implications for binding into the
therapeutic instrument itself, i.e. into the hospital, the pathogenic influences the instrument is intended to combat.

TABLE III
Participation in Games by Type of Patient

	Mean Game-day Ratios	*Mean Ages*
For all patients	·13	41
For those participating in games	·19	34
For those not participating	0	52
For the six highest participators	·39	30
For Insiders	·17	36
For Outsiders	·05	48
For Indeterminates	·15	38

Looking at the matter in another way, we may suggest that
unsophisticated and perhaps overworked personnel will tend to
foster patient cultures that contribute to their own security and
to job ease. The worst example of this can be seen in the old-
fashioned mental hospital where catatonic or dilapidated
patients were permitted to sit in indissoluble pairs on the
hospital floors or benches, as long as they did not bother the
help, until death separated them.

A final word on this section should emphasize that I do not
suggest that all patient cultures are contra-therapeutic. The preceding paragraphs merely describe one source and one case of
the genesis and reinforcement of a pathogenic patient–personnel culture.

In connection, once again, with the examination of the

insider and outsider groups, a word is necessary about the highest participants in games, patients T, U, N, P, H and L. Four of these are insiders. Within the insider group itself there was a group of 'deep insiders', as a clique, reinforced by the personnel through games. At the core of the clique, all females, were Mrs P and Miss N – rather good-looking, aggressively seductive younger women, both in close contact with reality, readily attracting the male attendants. Since the male attendants became involved in games more frequently with clique members than with other insiders, it is clear that in this respect also the hospital employees were reinforcing the patient social structure. In doing this, they were certainly selling even the other insiders short, for they did not play games as often with them as with members of the clique. Thus they were, by selecting the most reality-oriented group in the solarium, giving help to those who needed it least.

In this paper evidence has been presented to illustrate the way in which a socially patterned defect – to use Fromm's expression – has been dragged into the psychiatric milieu from the outer world and the perceptual characteristics of the defect utilized in the cultural patterning of space, as manifested in the distinction between insiders and outsiders. It is difficult, of course, to find a culture in the world where there is not some patterning into in- and out-groups, and where these exist they will naturally, in accordance with deep-going innate tendencies of the animal world, tend to distribute themselves in terms of natural or manufactured features of the environment. In any psychiatric environment that is therapeutically sensitive, however, personnel and patients must collaborate to ensure that this tendency to spatially structure the environment does not come to exercise lethal effects on the patients and undermine the effectiveness of the personnel.

2

When we look at the insider–outsider dichotomy from one point of view, it appears that the division represents simply a special case of the tendency of humans to create such groups and to arrange them around any environmental feature available. When we consider, however, that the underlying assumption of present-day institutional research is that behaviours taking place in an institution are also expressions of the properties of the institution itself, we are compelled to remove our eyes for a moment from the patient–personnel relations in the insider–outsider division and look more closely at the institution as a whole. When we do that, we perceive the following: 1. the psychiatric ward was just one of two such wards in a very large medical centre; 2. the nursing service was directed by a woman whose training was some twenty years in her background and, furthermore, was in medical nursing; 3. almost all of the nurses on the psychiatric service were recent trainees from the school of nursing of the hospital; and 4. the School of Nursing and the director of nursing services were antagonistic. Analysis will show that these circumstances played an important part in removing the nurses from interaction with the patients, and, thus in reducing the personnel available to the patients.

Observation of non-routine patient–personnel interaction[2] (Tables IV and V) shows that the nurses spent the least time with the patients. This is striking in view of the fact that in my interviews on nurse functions the response of psychiatric-nurse trainees was strongly in the direction of association with the patients. The contrast between the nurses and other personnel in time spent with patients becomes even more striking when it is realized that the nurses outnumbered attendants in the morn-

2. Not included in the tables are responses of the personnel to requests ('May I please have my glasses?' 'May I have a glass of orange juice?'), efforts to control the patients ('Time for OT, ladies!'), or dancing.

ings and were about equal to them in number in the afternoon–evening shift. The number of students varied, though at times they outnumbered the nurses.[3]

TABLE IV
Frequency of Non-Routine Interaction of Nurses, Students, and Attendants with Patients

Category of Personnel	Number of Times Observed in Verbal Interaction	Number of Times Observed in Games	Totals
Student	25	25	50
Nurse	46	1	47
Attendant	32	35	67
Totals	103	61	164

TABLE V
Number and Duration of Verbal Interaction between Personnel and Patients

Category of Personnel	Time in Seconds			Time in Minutes				One Hour or More	Totals
	1–5	6–30	31–59	1–2	3–5	6–10	11–59		
Student	3	4	2	1	1		2	1	14
Attendant	2	1	2						5
Nurse	3	9	9	3	4	1	1		30
Totals	8	14	13	4	5	1	3	1	49

A time analysis of *verbal* interaction of personnel with patients[4] demonstrates that time spent by personnel with patients in verbal interchanges not associated with games tended to be short, and that the time spent in the bulk of such interchanges was less than a minute (see Table V). But over and above the positive frequencies of contacts of nurses with patients is the negative fact of the *absence* of contact. That is to

3. There were four nurses on the 7 a.m. to 3 p.m. shift and two on the 3 to 11 shift; there were two attendants on the 7 to 3 shift and three on the 3 to 11 shift.
4. Since time was not recorded for all interactions, the number of verbal interactions analysed in Table V is smaller than the total in the second column in Table IV.

say, during the sixty-five hours of observation, the over-whelming bulk of it conducted while patients were awake and active, nurses were seen in verbal interaction with patients only forty-six times aside from routine contacts.

The crucial question to be answered is: what kept the nurses away from the patients? Spontaneous opinions obtained in interviews, at conferences, and as chance remarks contribute to an answer to the question:

1. *Nurse:* Complains of being a 'chart' nurse (i.e. spending her time charting); she can't spend time with the patients.

2. *Nurse:* Complains of having to keep the place clean instead of taking care of patients.

3. *Physician:* 'We've got so many damn charts we can't tell what's wrong with the patient any more.'

4. *Nurse:* 'When you go off duty, they don't know whether you have spent time with the patients, but they *do* know whether you have written in the chart.'

5. *Nurse:* 'Only students talk to patients. Graduates (i.e. staff nurses) are always in the office.'

6. *Nurse:* 'If you have to write the Kardex as well as the report, we'll be sitting in the office all the time.'

7. *Nurse:* 'If the powers that be see a graduate playing with the patients, they think we have too many nurses.'

8. *Nurse:* 'The patients have nothing to do between 7 and 9 p.m. and the nurse should be with the patient, but this is also the time to chart if you want to get off on time; and I've done it a few times myself . . .'

9. *Nurses*
   (at
   conference): (a) Administration considers time spent with
   patients loafing;
   (b) There is too much charting;
   (c) Dr Henry feels more comfortable with
   the patients than we do.

Since six of nine informants referred to excessive record keeping in spite of the presence of a ward clerk, we ought to have a look at the amount of charting, slip and order-sheet filling-out, and general record keeping the nurses were required to do. My list shows thirty-five different charts, slips, sheets, reports, notes, blanks, cards, and permits that had to be filled out or accounted for by the nurses (see Table VI). As one nurse put it, 'Even if the nurse does not have to fill out the chart or sheet, it's just as much trouble to see that they are there.'

The importance attached to the clerical work had, of course, an important effect on nurse functioning. This effect is suggested by the remark of one nurse: 'When you go off duty, they don't know whether you have spent time with the patients, but they do know whether you have written in the chart.' This raises the important ancillary problem of the *hidden deficit*, which may be stated as follows: when a subordinate worker has a choice of tasks of unequal visibility, he will tend to perform the task of greater visibility and neglect the task of lower visibility – visibility referring, of course, not to what the worker sees, but rather to what his supervisor can see. The property of 'visibility', however, is related to the values of a social system: what we look for are the things we value most. This brings up the matter of the values of the hospital.

In the present setting the task of the nurse was most generally discussed in terms of routine by the line departments other than the Department of Psychiatry. The following extract from a long interview with an important executive who was in close contact with the nursing staff is typical:

Miss Yor should be left free to supervise, to see that things get done. To see that the patients are fed, kept clean, that they get medication, and attend to the sanitation of the wards . . . When the students leave to go to class, there might be only two nurses on, and they have to write up all the charts and see that the patients are sent to the X-ray room and that they go to O.T. And if the secretary is tied up, Miss Yor has to answer the phone; there are reports to write . . . *Miss Sac is quite good. She has been supervising cleaning of the ward by the orderlies, and she helps with the charting*; and while Miss Yor is gone she has been making the assignments . . . The nurses have to see that the patient is taken care of and that the rooms are in order . . . all this must be written down on the assignment sheet.

In all this solicitude for the physical well-being of the patient, and care that the prescribed routines be carried out, we perhaps see the values of the general hospital – which are oriented toward physical care and asepsis – grafted or imposed on a psychiatric service. If we revert now to the original problem of the insiders and outsiders, we can perceive that phenomenon as in part an expression of the properties of the total hospital

TABLE VI
Records that Nurses Must Complete or Keep in Order

Chart	*How Often Filled Out*
1. EST	Every time shock is given to the patient.
2. Initial order sheet	Whenever an order is changed.
*3. Doctor's work sheet	Nurses have nothing to do with this.
4. Sleep chart	Every night.
5. Graphic	Several times a day, depending on patient.
6. Standing order sheet	Every time a new order is given.
7. Medication and treatment	Several times a day.
8. Nurse's note	At least two times a shift.
9. History sheets – progress notes	Nurses do not fill these out, but if patient is on daily urine analysis or blood counts, the nurses or the ward secretary must copy them.

Chart	How Often Filled Out
*10. Typed history sheets	Nurses do not fill them out.
*11. Physical examination sheet	Nurses do not fill them out.
12. Admission laboratory data	If the ward secretary does not fill out this sheet, the assistant head nurse does.
*13. Reiter-shock permit	Nurses do not fill them out.
*14. EST permit	Nurses do not fill them out.
*15. IST permit	Nurses do not fill them out.
16. Hospital-ward report	Made out by one person once each shift. If an accident occurs, this report must be drawn up by five people: the one who saw the accident occur; the physician; the head nurse; the supervisor; the superintendent.
18. Narcotic sheets	Once each shift.
19. Psychiatric-ward report	Once each shift.
20. Clina-test sheets	Must be filled out for diabetes four times in 24 hours.
21. Drug-supply slip	Once each shift.
22. Ward-supply slip	Once a week.
23. Diet slips	Three times a day.
24. Linen slips	Once a day.
25. Supply requisitions	Three or four times a day.
26. Charge slips (for treatments)	Once a day.
27. Transport, discharge, and transfer sheets	As needed.
28. Laboratory slips (including X-ray)	There are generally one or two patients a day for whom this must be done.
29. Prescription blanks	By one to three people – five or ten a day.
30. Kardex cards	Once a day.
31. Diet slip #2 (this slip records how much and what a patient eats)	One person does this three times a day (for each meal) for all patients.
32. Assignment sheets	By head nurse twice a day.
*33. Time slips	By ward secretary.
*34. Hours sheet	By ward secretary once a week.
35. Medicine chart	Made out as needed by whoever takes the order.

* Sheets not filled out by nurse.

system. The heavy emphasis on routines and clerical work withdrew the nurses from interaction with the patients; indeed the value system of the general hospital tended to penalize the nurse who spent time with patients. The withdrawing of the nurses from the patients in this way reduced the number of trained personnel available to the patients. The result was a general neglect of the psychotherapeutic aspects of the unit. Ward life was left to chance, and although patients spent their time out in the hallway day in and day out the nurses were too busy with routines to know or care about it. On this unit, nurses had to ask the attendants about the patients in order to write their reports.[5]

Nurses' preoccupation with the routines of clerical work and housekeeping, however, had a further source – in the conflict between the director of nursing and the School of Nursing over who was to control the unit and the behaviour of the psychiatric nurses. This silent struggle, in which neither side talked to the other, was waged through the nurses, who, while loyal to the School of Nursing, were yet threatened by the ultimate hiring and firing power of the director of nursing, a power made even more threatening by the director's antago-nism to the school. What we witness, then, on this unit is a veritable flight of the nurses from the patients and the leaving of the development of the milieu largely to chance[6] and to drift. The final result of the antagonism between the director of nursing services and the School of Nursing was that the school was removed as a training centre for graduate nurses from this hospital and the hospital set up its own.

In this section I have attempted to point to some of the ways

5. The fact that the attendants were the nurses' defenders against agitated patients tended to make the nurses reluctant to exert control over the attendants.

6. This phenomenon was, in part, also an expression of the lack of interest of the Department of Psychiatry in manipulating the ward as a therapeutic milieu.

in which the total organization of the hospital affected the relations between personnel and patients and contributed to the formation of the interesting space-oriented division of the patients into insiders and outsiders. In doing this I indicated that the values of the director of nursing were quite different from those of the psychiatric training given by the School of Nursing, and that the director of nursing won out because of her power to hire and fire and because the nurses, most of them students of the School of Nursing, were fearful of the antagonism between the director and the school. It was suggested that the encystment of the nurses within their cocoon of charts and routines, an isolation rendered even tighter by the institutional conflict, resulted in the nurses' almost total withdrawal from the patients and a consequent policy of drift. Thus the situation of the nurses does not account for the *specific* division of the patient population into in- and outsiders; it accounts, rather, for an apathy that permitted much in the milieu to go unattended. Meanwhile it is scarcely necessary to point out that a deluge of paper work has suffocated many nursing abilities everywhere, quite apart from any institutional antagonism. Even had the director and the School of Nursing been on good terms, the ideology of psychotherapeutic care that the nurses received in training could not have survived the values of the general hospital backed by the awesome power to hire, to fire, and to recommend.

Summary and Conclusions

Any group of human beings will tend to arrange itself in space in line with culturally determined perceptions of that space. This is just as true of the hordes of Australian natives as it is of patients in a psychiatric hospital. In the institutions of our own culture all the spatial arrangements within their four walls will be determined by the values of the total culture, and an *uncontrolled* psychiatric environment will inevitably drift into spatial arrangements ingenuously reflecting the values of the outer world. The problem of *control*, however – the problem of whether *drift* itself shall or shall not occur – is related to the alertness and sensitivity of the staff. And, in turn, that alertness and sensitivity are related in a strictly deterministic way to the power-backed values within the total institution.

4. A Theory for an Anthropological Analysis of American Culture*

A theory for an anthropological analysis of *American* culture cannot be a general theory of *culture*, because it is a theory of a particular culture; and it cannot be a theory that will cover all aspects of American culture because the culture is too complex to be grasped by a single theory, and because the units with which we deal are not constants – are not capable of complete definition, like, for example, a cubic centimetre of water. When we treat the analysis of culture as if we were dealing with constants, we suffer from the illusion of rigour; more often it is scientific *rigor mortis*. In spite of these reservations, however, good theories of culture usually do have some generalizing capabilities.

Another limitation in all theories of culture inheres in the circumstance that they have to be directed towards a particular problem. A theory that might explain, let us say, Crevecouer's view of eighteenth-century America would not help to understand why Ben Franklin in his autobiography barely mentions his wife. Thus different aspects of life call for different theoretical formulations. Theories of culture also have limitations imposed by the historic epoch in which they are conceived: mid-nineteenth-century theories of capitalism are not adequate to the contemporary variety. When we formulate a theory

* Reprinted from *Anthropological Quarterly*, Vol. XXXIX, No. 2, April 1966.

about a contemporary culture, therefore, we should take account of the conditions prevailing at the moment. A theory of a culture is thus time-bound and is ordinarily formulated in order to account for particular phenomena within a limited time range. The more a single theory of culture attempts to explain, the more vacuous it is likely to become: hence we speak of the inverse ratio between extension and precision; the more a theory of culture covers the less it enables us to say about any particular. Meanwhile the obverse is not true, viz., that the more limited the theory the greater its power to explain a narrow phenomenon, for it is often only through the effort to extend the theory beyond the initial object that new light is shed on the old problem.

The development of a theory of culture cannot occur without arbitrariness, for we have no way of determining objectively – as the physicists now have, for example – the fundamental building blocks of the human universe, culture. But within this arbitrariness there are just two possible theory choices, the idealist and the materialist; we try to construct a theory either on the basis of logical or metaphysical categories or on the basis of some material phenomenon like the economic system, the environment, etc. Anthropology has throughout its historic course followed the latter method and usually has either reacted violently against theories stressing non-material factors or has ignored them. Now, however, with the rise of the school of ethnoscience, anthropology is developing the possibility of a real controversy between idealists and materialists. Between the two, meanwhile, stand the energists, neither flesh nor fowl, for whom Energy has become a demon attached to everything and nothing.

With these considerations in the back of my mind and with some recklessness, I set myself to construct an anthropological theory of American culture that would help me explain the contemporary character of our people. Or, to put it more candidly, I had a certain view of the character of Americans. I needed a theory to account for the qualities I perceived, and I had a predisposition to materialist formulations. I shall be more candid still: there are many qualities I dislike in myself and many I lament in my fellows, and I wished to account for them. As one reviews what might be called the *literature of explanation* from Plato to Freud, Marx, Kierkegaard and Heidegger, one perceives that all formulations of man or his society are motivated by such simple considerations. It may be possible to achieve some objectivity in discussing remote peoples in the mountains of New Guinea, but when we are at home we are all fishmongers, housewives and old men arguing around the cracker barrel.

The question now is: what is an anthropological theory? In cultural anthropology we generally think of an anthropological theory as holistic. As one reads anthropological monographs, however, one perceives that generally they do not deal with wholes. In our discipline a holistic theory is not a theory of the whole but rather an open theory that aims at the establishment of a network of relationships. As a matter of fact, in cultural anthropological writings we must speak of a holistic *approach* rather than of a holistic theory, for the theory of relationship is never given. Considering the gross nature of the data with which we cope it is unlikely that a general theory of relationship could ever be given. When one deals with relationships among cultural facts as gross as economic structure, kinship, religious ideas and practices, and so on, one is limited by the fact that there is no device, logical or mechanical, to aid in proving that a relationship actually exists. Actually then, what determines whether the interpretation of a culture is judged to be well or poorly done are the cultural conventions of the discipline.

An anthropological formulation is not a factor formulation, i.e. a formulation in which a limited number of factors, or sometimes only one factor, are selected as basic and all others are derived from them. In the human disciplines good examples of factor theories are orthodox psychoanalysis and learning theory.

The former is based on sexuality and the latter on reinforcement. Thus anthropological approaches are not reductionist. They rest on naturalistic inference, or better, informed guesswork, rather than on an assumption of underlying factors that always have the same effects. Educated guessing based on the broadest possible knowledge of the realities available is, meanwhile, characteristic of all the human disciplines. Economics, since it has developed many measuring instruments, deals with a relatively limited phenomenon, has long historic records and has available vast accumulations of observations, is least subject to guesswork among the human disciplines, but even there we know full well how many times the economists are mistaken. Psychology, to the extent that it is not subject to guessing, is not a human discipline but rather an animal one, based largely on rats and pigeons.

Another characteristic of the holistic approach in anthropology is the insistence that all parameters be made explicit. For example, no anthropologist could be satisfied with a pure demand–supply explanation of price, but would insist that the fact that the relation among the factors is characteristic only of a private-enterprise economy be made explicit. He would also insist that, to the degree that the relationship held, it was true of a competitive culture only, where maximization of return was a value, that it assumed the existence of 'perfect competition', and so on. In this, I believe, we differ from all the other human disciplines. In this also we were – as ignoramuses, of course – far advanced in scientific thinking. Unaware of our own sophistication, we have nevertheless always insisted on what is now the sign of sophisticated science, to wit, that at all times all parameters of a discussion be made explicit.

A further characteristic of cultural anthropology is shared with history. This is the emphasis on a sequence of events, and especially on the historic moment. That is to say, in ethnographic studies what we stress is the flow of time through people or the flow of people, as they interact, through time;

and the critical moment at which something happens – when the *kula* valuable finally changes hands, when the Murngin boy is circumcised, when the hank of sennit is handed over to the sister's husband in Tikopia, and so on. To the degree that what we consider in cultural anthropology is always a transaction, appearing and vanishing in a critical moment, we are historical. That, it seems to me, has always been the deeper meaning of history in anthropology whether we are dealing with Kroeber, Boas or Benedict.

The next question is: what do I mean by national character? *By national character I mean a group of interrelated motivations, values and feelings prevailing among a people.* I think of these as distributed in a population somewhat in the way physical characteristics are. For example, there is a prevalence among Swedes of long heads, long faces, blond hair and blue eyes, but not every Swede is long-headed, long-faced, blond and blue-eyed. Nevertheless these traits are scattered widely enough among the Swedish population to give it a distinctive character. Similar considerations apply to the analysis of national character: certain traits of character – certain motivations, values and feelings – are observed among the people of a nation but *not all the traits are assumed to be present in everybody, nor are they assumed to be present in the same strength*. People within cultural and national boundaries must share certain traits of character, otherwise the whole idea of cultural determinism becomes meaningless. But there must be widespread sharing of character traits also in order that there be some basis for understanding and predicting behaviour in everyday life. Finally the assumption that there is a bundle of shared character traits in a population which makes it possible for people to make reasonable predictions about each other does not deny the existence of those traits elsewhere, especially if the same cultural tradition is shared. After all, the motivations of David and Saul are clear to us even today, and that is one of the principal reasons why Bible stories still make sense.

I turn now to a recent expression of national character – the language used by President Lyndon B. Johnson in his first budget message. His words, directed to the entire population of the United States, embody correct assumptions about our national character. The first selections are from his first message as printed in the *New York Times,* 22 January 1964. The first paragraph reads as follows:

The preparation of this budget was the first major task to confront me as a President, and it has been a heavy one. Many decisions of great importance have had to be made in a brief span of weeks. I have done my best, and I am satisfied that the budget which I am sending to the Congress will advance our Nation toward greater national security, a stronger economy, and realization of the American dream of individual security and equal opportunity for all our people.

Thus in the first place the President asks for our sympathy, saying he has worked hard and done his best with a heavy task and that he did not have much time. At the same time, by asking our sympathy, he equalizes status difference. He then tells us that we are going to be more secure than ever against outside enemies, that we are going to be stronger than ever and that our American dream is going to be closer to realization. It seems scarcely necessary to point out that this language ministers to many yearnings in the American character. What is most interesting, however, is that the language makes a personal appeal – the President's burdens have been heavy, he has worked hard, the time has been short – to the intimate sympathies of the American people, sympathies assumed to be readily available to public figures and to be necessary to the stability in office of public men.

Since the message is too long for extensive quotes, I would simply mention here that there are references in it to the values of strength, progress, human compassion (paragraph 2) and to challenges and opportunities (paragraph 3), which clearly make assumptions about our national character, and which indeed will readily be recognized as important features of it.

By 1965 the President was feeling more secure and the remarks introducing the budget (the *New York Times*, 26 January 1965) are briefer, but we are still told how difficult matters are. I skip over the very brief introduction, to the fourth paragraph where the President says:

It is a budget of *opportunity* and *sacrifice*. It begins to grasp the *opportunities* of the *Great Society*. It is *restrained* by the *sacrifices* we must continue to make in order to keep our defences *strong* and *flexible*.

This budget provides reasonably for our needs. It is *not extravagant*. Neither is it *miserly* . . .

The Great Society must be a *bold* society. It must not fear to meet new *challenges*. It must not fail to *seize new opportunities*.

The Great Society must be a *compassionate* society. It must always be *responsive* to human needs.

The Great Society must be an *efficient* society . . . [Italics supplied]

I have italicized the value words that express well-known components of our national character.

In spite of the President's words, it should come as no surprise to people of our national character, that the largest and most detailed section of the budget is *National Defence*. Meanwhile it seems unnecessary to labour the point that the words are likely to stimulate strong positive responses in most Americans because their character contains the motivations and the values complementary to the words.

Before closing this introduction I shall quote from another document – *Life* magazine's (7 May 1965) article on Roger Miller, the popular country music singer. Speaking of Miller's most famous song, the article says:

It's only a little song about the pleasures – and pain – of being a bum, about the unfettered life of a fellow who sleeps in four-bit hotel rooms, picks up half-smoked stogies, and knows every train engineer by name. But the beat of *King of the Road* is catchy, the melody infectious, and the lyrics ring appealingly to anybody who feels closed in and would like to get out and breathe a little. Aimed originally at the hillbilly market, *King of the Road* has suddenly sold more than a million copies to become the most popular tune in America.

Ready sympathy, though not necessarily help, for the lonely and the down-trodden, and the feeling of being hemmed in; the longing to be foot-loose and not tied down are the traits, common enough in the American character, that make this 'the most popular tune in America' this month.

I turn now from these examples of popular materials which are based on the assumption of widespread character traits, to a more technical examination of theoretical issues bearing on the general anthropological analysis of the United States and its relation to personality.

Economy and Character

My book, *Culture against Man*, is an essay in culture and personality in which the course of the development of the argument is set by the assumption that the causes of certain traits of American character are to be sought in the economic system – in itself no revolutionary idea. The economic system is construed as the system of private enterprise with its attendant drives and values. For the sake of clear presentation of the problem, I divided socially determined motivations into two broad classes, values and drives. The latter were defined as motivations tending to maximize the economy and personal status within its organizations; and the former were defined as motivations tending to maximize satisfaction in interpersonal relations as idealized in family and friendship.[1] Fundamentally

1. In *Culture against Man* (1963, pp. 13–14) I stated my position as follows: 'Ours is a driven culture. It is driven on by its achievement, competitive, profit and mobility drives, and by the drives for security and a higher standard of living. Above all, it is driven by expansiveness . . . Side by side with these drives is another group of urges, such as gentleness, kindness, and generosity, which I shall call values . . . Values and drives – other than physiological drives – are both creations of the culture, but in

the argument is simple, viz., that the economic system has certain consequences for personality and that the consequences and the emergent personality traits can be detected in all phases of culture. I did not consider the possibility that personality determines institutions because this leaves the source of the personality traits unaccounted for; and I spoke of personality traits rather than of personality configurations, because while single traits are readily identified in a national population, personality configurations vary too much from individual to individual.

In order to discuss the American economic system, it was necessary to have a good account and a reasonable theory of it, and inasmuch as my view of the American economy had been fundamentally influenced by *The Structure of the American Economy*, prepared by a committee of technicians and scholars under the chairmanship of Gardner Means, during the second presidential term of Franklin Roosevelt for the purpose of assisting in economic reform, it was reasonable to take that document for my theoretical foundation. It will be recalled that during the depths of the depression more than a quarter of the labour force in this country was unemployed, the economy was on the verge of total collapse and revolution seemed a real possibility, as millions lacked bare necessities. There was good reason therefore for an honest account of the economy to be produced in order to prevent revolution and to serve as a foundation for reform.

Accompanying *The Structure of the American Economy* was a

---

the lives of Americans, and, indeed, of all 'Western' men and women, they play very different roles. A value is something we consider good; something we always want our wives, husbands, parents and children to express to us, to shower on us when we are gay, to tender to us when we are miserable. Love, kindness, quietness, contentment, fun, frankness, honesty, decency, relaxation, simplicity belong here... Drives are what urge us blindly into getting bigger... Drives belong to the occupational world; values to the world of the family and friendly intimacy.'

covering letter to the President, signed by several cabinet members and other high government officials, which states that, 'This document is the first major attempt to show the interrelations of the economic forces which determine the use of our natural resources.' Thus the first words of the report compel the attention of the anthropologist because of the use of his own magical expression 'interrelation'! The covering letter tells us, by implication, that we are not to read a self-limiting disquisition on the maximization of prices or production, but an open analysis of the interrelation of a complex of factors. Proceeding to the Preface we read:

In this report on *The Structure of the American Economy* an effort is made to bring the major aspects of the national economy into focus so as to emphasize the organic character of the process whereby the Nation's resources are employed to provide useful commodities and services. This emphasis on organization requires that the national community be treated as a single functioning whole in such a way that every phase of human activity is covered insofar as it involves the use of resources.

I am sure that those who still believe that cultural anthropology is indeed the study of culture 'as a single functioning whole' cannot but be attracted to this formulation. I do not know whether the array of experts who contributed to the preparation of this document had read Malinowski, Durkheim, Dilthey, or R. Benedict, but surely the preface and the entire volume express their spirit.

Having cited the covering letter and the Preface, let us now turn to the Introduction. A major concern of the book is to state the causes and consequences of the great depression and to suggest ways of avoiding another. The report therefore discusses the enormous loss in production and income, but continues as follows (p. 3):

Even more basically significant is the individual frustration resulting from the inability to find effective use for one's skills. Without the satisfaction of useful activity, without the sense of security in a job well done, most men lose some of their self-reliance and some of their ability to be productive.

It is clear that the economists, who have built up in this book, with its 18 Appendixes, an array of tables, diagrams, charts, maps, and models that would gratify the most exacting, acknowledge that there are such personality characteristics as 'individual frustration', the desire to be effective, the satisfaction in work, a 'sense of security' and self-reliance, and that these are affected radically by the economic system. One may then ask, 'If these traits are so closely related to the economic structure, why not others?'

Turning at last to the major analysis of this report, which begins with the second chapter, we see that the authors, in the very first sentence, place the *consumer* in the centre of the economic structure, saying, 'Basic to the structure of the American economy are the wants of the consumers.' Thus the consumer is placed in the centre of the economic system and not price, profit or production. From one point of view the theory advanced in *The Structure of the American Economy* places the *burden* of economic survival on the consumer; from another it makes clear that unless there are consumers, i.e. *individuals* with money in their pockets to buy, the economy has no basis. From this one may make the reasonable inference that individuals have to learn well how and what to consume, must be given the possibility of consuming, must be induced to buy and convinced not to save too much. This is true even though the system rests fundamentally on the profit motive and consumers are merely instruments through which profit is realized. What I have begun to do here is to take conclusions derived from study of the economic system and extend them logically to a point where they can be used for the analysis of national character. What this procedure does is simply *put the economic necessity* into human beings and ask, 'What *human* qualities must the human being have in order to achieve the requirements of the *system*?' Depending on the point of view it is either a tautology or an iron law that character traits must match system requirements. The answer to the question should always be given in the most primitive type of inferences, for example, since most traits of *Homo sapiens* are learnt, one has to learn how to consume, i.e., in our culture, how to buy. If consumer wants are the basis of the economy, the consumers must also be taught to want enough to support the economy. No other type of person is conceivable in such a system. Since, if consumers are to express their wants, they have to be given the wherewithal to buy, this implies the necessity of raising real wages. But if consumers are to express wants adequate to support an economy such as ours, they cannot save too much; as a matter of fact, they must be taught to dissave. Actually not personality theory but only rather simple logic is necessary to arrive at these conclusions. Thus a wanting, dissaving *character* is necessary in order to carry out the requirements of consumption and dissaving in our culture. In other words, austerity is not wanted. But if austerity is not wanted then the institutions – such as the established churches – which, in the past have sustained the ideals of austerity must either recede into the background or take on the characteristics of institutions devoted to maintaining the required level of consumption.

Summarizing up to this point: in an expanding economy based on consumer wants, every effort must be made to place the standard of living in the centre of public and private consideration, and every effort must therefore be bent to remove material and psychological impediments to consumption. Hence, rather than feelings of restraint, feelings of letting-go must be in the ascendant, and the institutions supporting restraint must recede into the background and give way to their opposite.

The authors of *The Structure of the American Economy* give us a precise analysis of consumer wants. These data are obtained simply by taking advantage of the patterned records maintained by the Bureau of Labor Statistics over a period of many years, and based on carefully controlled interviews with consumers. From Chart IV 'Expenditures of American Consumers', p. 11, and Table I – 'Effect of size of income on direction of expenditure – Comparison of expenditure of 1 million dollars by consumers at 2 different levels of income', p. 11, it is apparent that the expenditures of consumers fall into a pattern; but what is most illuminating is Table III 'Effect of level of consumer expenditures on the direction of expenditures', on p. 14, which projects the probabilities of American consumer expenditures at different levels of national income. Discussing the table the book states (p. 15):

The most striking feature of Table III is the apparent lack of any indication of a limit to any of the (consumer) wants reflected in the items (in the table). At the highest level of expenditure, for every one of the separate items there would be a great increase in expenditure over the lowest . . .

For each major category of consumption, the structure of wants appears to be such that a big lift in consumer expenditures would create a greatly increased domestic market for every broad class of products.

The table and its discussion are momentous, for the clear implication is that since there are no limits to consumer wants, Americans, as consumers, are insatiable, for that indeed is what no limit on wants means. 'Consumer wants' is generally interpreted to mean only the items included in the Retail Price Index of the Bureau of Labor Statistics and these items have been added to from time to time, as new wants have appeared. The wants reflected in the index are almost entirely egoistic ones – like clothing, food, housing, and so on – that have to do with personal gratification. Meanwhile it is clear that the expression 'personal gratification' is not susceptible of any rigorous definition. For example, I might get a great deal of personal gratification out of knowing that we have put a man on the moon. Hence, while I am not yet ready to extend the idea of insatiability to space, there is nothing logical in the way of my doing so.

The statistical foundation for the inference that Americans – who are probably no different from the rest of modern men in this respect – are insatiable, strengthens the basis for the view that the desire for impulse release in the direction of consumption must be a fundamental feature of American personality. At the end of this chapter the authors, after conducting the reader through the usual painstaking statistical analysis, make the following statement:

> The indications are clear that American consumers, if they had sufficient money income, would constitute a market sufficient to absorb all the production which American industry has the resources to turn out.

While the rise in real wages since 1939 has made possible the realization of the potentialities expressed in this passage, the rise has been accomplished, as we all know, largely through an enormous increase in expenditures for armaments; for these have come back to workers in increased wages, which in turn have gone into continuous increases in consumption. However, the increases have not been accomplished without stimulation from advertising and alterations in education. It is also true that the *possibility* of an American market sufficient to absorb all the production of American industry is a *necessity* because of the poverty of the rest of the world and its consequent inability to absorb our exports. That is to say an American *possibility* is an American *necessity* because much of the rest of the world is too poor to buy what we produce at the prices we are willing to sell them. Thus starting from a finding based on an economic analysis, I arrive at a somewhat expanded conclusion.

The explanation of the unavailability of our exports does not end here, however. The very success the American economy has had in raising profits and the living standard has, by increasing the price of what we produce, helped to price our goods out of much of the foreign market.[2] Meanwhile the fact that more than half the federal budget goes into armaments places an enormous amount of armaments-derived wages in the hands of consumption units, thus exercising further upward pressure on prices and making our goods even less accessible outside the country. A further important circumstance compelling us to consume at home is the curtailment or cutting off of trade with communist countries.

Thus the statement 'that American consumers . . . would constitute a market sufficient to absorb all the production which American industry has the resources to turn out' has to be modified in two respects. The first is that this market has not really been tested, because so much of what is produced is not available to consumers; and second that what *is* available literally *has* to be consumed at home. It follows that, in view of the fact that our industrial capacity is the greatest in the world, Americans must be trained to consume more than anybody else in the world.

We are not finished, however, even yet, with the complex problem of pressure to consume. There are fundamentally two types of consumption – consumption in the private and consumption in the public sectors. Consumption in the private sector is essentially egoistic consumption. Consumption in the public sector pertains to schools, roads, water purification, hospitals, defence, space and so on. All governments have to calculate how much can be exacted in taxes for public consumption; that is to say, how much taxation people will tolerate. This is usually done by guesswork; and in our country taxes are exacted by a democratic combination of salesmanship and coercion. But taxes for the public sector must always compete with wants in the private sector. What democratic governments

2. The decline of our exports from 16 per cent of total production in 1919 to about 4 per cent in 1960, including armaments, paces the rise in our living standard and the growth of a war industry as an essential factor in the economy.

do is try to *make the expenditure of tax money appear as if they were expenditures for egoistic consumption*. However, this often cannot be done, particularly in the area of armaments. What the United States government has done, however, is produce such domestic euphoria through vast expenditures on defence and space that they have *the psychological effect of egoistic consumption*. Paradoxically every nickel the government spends on missiles and capsules is money in the consumer's pocket. Thus the government buys off consumer reluctance to pay taxes by insuring him an increase in egoistic consumption through the pecuniary euphoria pumped into the economy by expenditures for weapons and space. In this way further inducements to egoistic consumption are offered. In the meanwhile space is widely advertised.

We must remember, meanwhile, that the euphoria has its origins in fear – fear of the communist block. This being the case, it is quite correct to say that we grow fat with fear; that consumption euphoria is based on international fear. Hence it is also correct to say that the consequences of a fearless society cannot but be economically dysphoric, and hence there is a functional utility in fostering fear. Or, put another way, there is no *pressing necessity* for allaying it. Meanwhile the fear is narcotized – and therefore sustained – by consumption euphoria: if someone injects you with morphine you forget the pain of cancer.

So far the argument has been logical, and based on inescapable economic conditions. I shall now, however, press on to another, more speculative area, where I shall use psychoanalysis, which is a different theory. When fear is present *Homo sapiens* can attack his enemy – which we try to do on an institutional level through armed force; he can fly from the enemy, which we do not do; or he can seek to narcotize his fear. Impulse release[3] via sexual-

3. In *Culture against Man* I use this expression for acts of self-indulgence – eating, sex, having fun, buying lots of good things, etc.; in other words, anything that is the opposite of self-restraint. I would also include, how-

ity, eating, and in general having a good time, are characteristic ways of doing this. Hence, we speculate, fear may lead to impulse release and thus indirectly make its contribution to consumption.

I turn now to a different dimension of the structure of the American economy: the factors making up the structure. These are natural resources, capital, technology, income and labour. In any contemporary economy these have to relate to one another in such a way that they are never in balance. If there were just enough resources to serve us for the day, the economy would soon stop, for it would run out of raw materials. Hence there must always be more than enough of them. Technology must always improve because of the competitive situation; productive plant must always increase in order to take care of the increasing population and the population must continue to grow – but not too fast – in order to man the growing productive plant. This will probably hold for a while in spite of automation. At the same time purchasing power must increase in order for consumption to remain at adequate levels. Enough has been said to indicate that an economy that relies on the right relationship among so many factors is inherently unstable; and the numerous depressions we have had throughout our history testify to this fact. This being the case, an array of phenomena emerges to control the instability. One is the giant corporation; another is diversification, which is simply another phase of corporate expansion. A third is the interlocking directorate which serves to regulate competition and corporate endeavours in general. A fourth is the interest group – a patterned network of mutual pecuniary interests made up of corporations, financial firms like Morgan-First National, Kuhn-Loeb, etc., and accounting and legal firms. All of this is set forth in *The Structure of the American Economy*. Such networks

---

ever, the release of hostile impulses. In this context impulse release is different from love, because the essence of love is not self-indulgence.

of legal, financial and industrial interests are careful regulating devices that guide large portions of the private sector. In addition government plays a determining role, because it uses its overshadowing power and benevolence to guide and control the private sector in such a way as to avoid economic plunges and abuses. The net result of such regulatory processes, from gigantic corporate networks to government benevolence, is to alter the personality requirements of the culture from eager, dynamic striving and pecuniary courage to quieter economic virtues centring largely around the type of personality so brilliantly described by Whyte in *The Organization Man*.

Here again I have inferred the probability of a certain personality trait from certain economic realities. The central issue always is simply that one transposes an economic – or any cultural condition – into a human being as a property of his character. When I say 'This is a carefully regulated *economy*' I can scarcely mean more than that this is an economic system in which the *conduct* of the members of the system is carefully regulated. It follows, then, that daring and eagerness, which represent the opposite of regulated conduct, are excluded as necessary factors in character, and would therefore tend to fade away in an epoch of carefully regulated economic life.

Up to this point I have been talking about contemporary America, but this cannot be done as if we had no past, as if the conditions of which I speak have no parallel in our own history. It is therefore necessary to do what is possible in a short paper in order to at least suggest the historical problem.

Historical Issues

As one reads Alexis de Tocqueville's *Democracy in America* one has the impression that one is reading about the character of contemporary Americans. The commitment to material pleasures, the fear of having an opinion different from one's neighbours, the lack of involvement in persons outside one's

family and narrow coterie of friends, the feeling that one stands
alone and that no one cares whether one lives or dies, are all
characteristics which we see widespread among us now and
which we deplore just as de Tocqueville did in 1831. These
characteristics are not described for America a hundred years
before de Tocqueville wrote. The question now is: how do we
explain the striking similarities between what de Tocqueville
observed and what we observe today? The general question is,
'If certain traits of character persist from century to century in
a given population, how is this to be explained?' Obviously the
question has far reaching importance, for the history of our
entire civilization gives examples of the amazing persistence of
values across centuries and millennia. Do values somehow have
a life of their own – whatever that means? But surely there is no
such thing as a value having a life of its own, like a person or a
bird. A clue to the answer is given, I think, by the differences
among the American of Revolutionary and of pre-Revolu-
tionary times and the American of de Tocqueville's day. The
conditions of life in America in the earlier periods were different
from those known to de Tocqueville. In the earlier period daring and independence were much more widely distributed in
the population because of the condition of the country and the
exigencies of the new farming life. At the same time there was
less to risk, for many who came here had nothing to lose but
their chains. By de Tocqueville's time cities had grown up and
more widespread vested interests already existed, with their
overshadowing threats to the survival of deviants. Hence the
opportunities for the emergence of the values and motivations
that de Tocqueville perceived. In de Tocqueville's day, meanwhile, the overriding factor in stifling deviant opinion was the
scramble for establishing one's economic footing, including
westward expansion, and the wresting of world markets from
the British. Any idea that threatened these two all-consuming
necessities had to be stifled. Nowadays there is an apparent
similarity between what we perceive through de Tocqueville's

writings and what we and our distinguished social critics see in us today; and the sustaining similarities in social conditions are the private-enterprise economy and antagonism to and fear of a foreign power, not Britain now but Russia and China. Thus in different periods of history similar traits of national character are sustained by similar social conditions, and when these change the national character will alter. However, it is likely that alteration means really that some persisting character traits recede into the background and others become salient.

The Cultural Manifold

As one reads about the history and the ideas of our cultural tradition one is struck by the apparent persistence through millennia of basic values, emotional responses and motivations. I cannot get out of my head the myth of the Hindu *yogi*, who stood so long in one place that he became like a tree, sprouting roots and branches, and who derived such power from austerity that the demons of Hindu mythology, in their wars, sought to enlist him on their side against their enemies. This is a beautiful picture of the amalgamation in one person of restraint, ambition and power so well known to our culture, particularly before the 1930s. Nor can I forget the ambition of David, the suspicion of Saul and the contempt of David's first wife, Michal, when he danced and showed off before the maidens of Israel as he brought the Ark home to Jerusalem. All of these people are understandable to me. Even the death of Socrates for misleading the children of the conforming aristocrats of his day is not surprising to me, nor his motivation in refusing to escape, for all these motivations, values and feelings are alive among us now. Such underlying complexes of motivations, values and feelings which persist under different sets of social conditions I call the *cultural manifold*. It may be surprising to some that even the argument about whether parents should be permissive or Spartan with their babies has long endured in our culture; and the problem of whether babies should be breast- or bottle-fed was as alive in eighteenth-century England as it is today. Thus in a great cultural tradition such as ours character traits and social institutions appear to persist. The traits of character can never quite disengage themselves from social conditions which reappear in different forms in different epochs; and the social conditions can never quite disengage themselves from the character traits, which appear over and over again with different emphases and under somewhat differing circumstances, because negation always lurks in the shadow of the affirmation. Passivity lurks in the shadow of action; cowardice in the shadow of courage; self-indulgence in the shadow of austerity; acquiescence in the shadow of resistance[4] – each standing ready for the bugle of changing circumstance. We do not know how the characterological features of our culture arose, for surely they had many sources, but we do know this, that throughout history they have appeared in different forms in different epochs and that the salience of one and the recession of another have been determined by changing social conditions.

The central issue is that values, motivations and feelings are the expression in inner life of the institutions of which one is a member. If this were not true there would be no relation between the two and a culture could not function. The statement, however, does not imply that institutions come first – as if in the beginning there was a void, an institution formed and from it emerged a social character. The institution of private property is expressed in the individual as a *belief* in it; but, since all

4. Passivity lurks in the shadow of action because so many who live by action at times long to relax and be passive; cowardice lurks in the shadow of courage because so many who live by their courage often wish to run away and hide; self-indulgence lurks in the shadow of austerity because many who live by restraint long to 'cut loose' and indulge themselves. Thus all civilizations store contradictions alongside their values; and particularly in the 'great civilizations', where the stresses within the dominant value orientations are so great, the contradiction may readily emerge under facilitating historic conditions, i.e. 'the bugle of changing circumstance'.

institutions reward some men and punish others, this is reflected in individuals as a dialectical contradiction between a belief in private property and a disbelief depending on whether one is rewarded or punished by the system. Those who live under a system of privilege will long for equality if the system punishes them, they will seize equality if they can get it and they will destroy privilege; while those who are rewarded by the system will hate equality and cut off the hands of those who reach for it.

Since institutional changes can never be disengaged from their expression in individuals, we always contend with the previously existing character; and institutional change does not leave the preceding character entirely altered, however radical the change may be. Thus character traits that seem to persist in a cultural tradition through eons, must always be analysed to see what it is that persists. The austerity of the Hindu of the myth I cited has little in common with the parsimony and restraint of the entrepreneur who wants to start a business; and, although yogi and entrepreneur express ambition also, the two strivings are different. The American desire for equality was not the same in early America as it is today, for today it is less a passion yearning in the flesh. Having achieved some form of equality, we are less intense about it than our ancestors 200 years ago, and to the degree that any semblance of that passion exists among us at all, it has been transferred from the white to the Negro race.

I close this paper with a glance back 260 years to the emergent democracy of America;[5]

Dudley[6] had lived much in England, had sat in Parliament, and had imbibed prerogative notions of government. He little relished the homely ways of New England and he bore himself somewhat haughtily. One December day in 1705, as he was driving along a

5. From Vernon Louis Parrington, *Main Currents in American Thought* (New York, 1927 and 1930).
6. Joseph Dudley, Royal Governor of New England.

country road with high snow drifts on each side, he met with two loads of wood. The chariot coming to a stop, Dudley thrust his head out of the window and bade the carters turn aside and make way for him; but they were inclined to argue the matter in view of the drifts. Words were multiplied, and one of the carters cried ... 'I am as good flesh and blood as you ... you may go out of the way.' In a rage the governor drew his sword and struck at the fellow, who snatched the sword and broke it.

This story illustrates the dialectic of equality and privilege: Dudley suffered from the ideology of equality, so had the carters thrown into gaol; they had found equality rewarding, suffered from the ideology of privilege and were imprisoned for the ideology of equality. Throughout history this dialectic – between reward and punishment, between revenge and martyrdom, has driven our culture on. It is a miserable way to progress; let us hope we will find a better way.

5. Vulnerability: Sources of Man's Fear in Himself and in Society*

Mankind is a vulnerable animal and suffers from feelings of vulnerability day in day out, awake and in his dreams. As a college teacher I am aware of the excruciating vulnerability of students; and my own sensation of vulnerability when I was a student will never leave me. I am remotely like the old professor in the movie *Wild Strawberries* who, at the peak of his fame, when he was about to receive the highest scholastic honour in the country, and a salute of cannons, had a dream the night before of failing an examination. It is not very long since I ceased to have such dreams: they are the primeval dreams of confronting life's test and failing.

I was once invited to participate in a symposium in which the participants were 'asked to take a new look at security systems in our society that prevent fluid functioning of the individual ego and creative adaptive response to new experience in both individuals and in the larger society'. Translated into vulgar English this means 'let us take a look at how people, in defending themselves against their fears, freeze and lose the ability to think freely and handle new situations'. Since the security system – or, better, the insecurity system – of us all is but a reflex of the insecurity – or vulnerability – of the social system as a whole, I took that as my starting point; for, if we want to

* This paper was an Assembly Talk given in Graham Chapel, Washington University, St Louis, Missouri, 2 December 1964.

know the roots of our *personal* feelings of vulnerability, let us look for them in the society in which we live. With this in mind, my first paragraphs explore the general nature of vulnerability in contemporary society.

Men feel vulnerable because their societies are contradictory within and because they are in danger of attack from enemies without. But they are also vulnerable from within their own society's protecting walls if they do not behave themselves, and they are vulnerable from within because of unacceptable impulses: because of guilt, intolerable hostilities and the feeling that they have sold their selves down the river to get ahead. It is along these four lines that I shall examine the feeling of vulnerability in our society. I begin with our economic system.

Vulnerability of the Economic System

In every epoch the sources of feelings of vulnerability are different. Now our feeling of vulnerability derives first of all from the instability of our economic system. The Great Depression, which held us in nightmare for ten years, and which my generation has transmitted as nightmare to its children, destroyed the dream of a self-regulating economy; so that even today, during the longest sustained economic boom in American history, only boneheads believe it will continue without lively efforts of government to prevent dislocations. Thus belief in economic vulnerability is economic wisdom and has come to supplant medieval notions of eternal, organic order and stability.

Western economies today are the most vulnerable in history. When I speak of a vulnerable economic system I do not refer to vulnerability from natural catastrophe, but to the vulnerability of the system to its own internal processes; in ours to the uncertainty of the adjustment among the factors of capital, production, distribution, labour, income, international balance of payments, and so on. In this sense anthropology has discovered no economic system on earth outside the West, in which such basic factors repeatedly move so seriously out of adjustment to one another that the economy temporarily collapses and people starve amid plenty. Economic vulnerability is thus a 'gift' to mankind of the 'higher civilization'; and wherever the western system is imposed on simpler economies they too become vulnerable.

It is this vulnerability that has altered the nature of private enterprise from the daring private-enterprise ideal of nineteenth-century economic tradition to the cautious corporate endeavours of the mid-twentieth, where huge expenditures for research, broad diversification and steady but moderate profit rates have become an expression of the shift to security from plunging in the hope of windfall returns.

Against the reality of economic vulnerability private enterprise has erected the international corporate network, whose primary object is the attainment of such power that it will be invulnerable to economic uncertainty; and, by this fear driven to diversify and develop systems of integration and corporate interlock, it has come about that 135 American corporations own one quarter of the assets of the world.[1] Yet even such power, unmatched in the history of our culture, is still inadequate to convince us that the economy is here to stay; and for this reason people must be taught to buy as they breathe; and the average person must be trained to feel a sense of pecuniary suffocation if he does not spend much of what he earns. A consequence of this is the suburban Saturday at the department store, where teenagers and younger go to while away the week-end, have rendezvous and perhaps pick up a free sample. Thus, transformed by the inner necessity of the vulnerable economic system to make everyone an automatic buyer, department stores have become the new museums of our culture. Not the Art Museum or the Museum of Natural His-

1. A. A. Berle, Jr.

tory, but the Museum of Dry Goods is the greatest centre of culture of our time. These children are learning much more that is worthwhile in the department store, much more that will save the culture from disaster, than they would in a conventional museum: they are learning how to buy, how to ransom us from the catastrophe of a vulnerable economic system.

The ramifications of the sensation of economic vulnerability are thus unexpected and difficult to estimate, but it is clear that an economic system that started out to express a desire for profit has become so concerned with becoming invulnerable that the intimate domestic and international effects of this have become incalculable.

It must also be borne in mind that there are no other economic systems on earth that have put such pressure on natural resources as those of the West – to such an extent indeed that the air we breathe and the water we drink are as much in danger of exhaustion through contamination as the basic materials of production. The repercussions of our vulnerability to loss of raw materials are felt in the farthest corners of the world, so that weak countries everywhere have become toys of the western powers as the latter struggle to replenish or hold on to basic raw materials. Our vulnerability to the production of other nations in a world economic system is so great that business sheds pecuniary tears on the financial pages of the *New York Times* over imports of textiles or galoshes, meat, steel and glass from Europe, and so on, and the tariff, the *protective tariff*, has never lost its vigour as a political and international issue. Finally our vulnerability to loss of fields for investment of our economic surplus does not cease to project us into armed conflict.

Life and Prestige

As one surveys economic systems throughout the non-industrialized world and throughout history, one is struck by a surprising phenomenon: that in the developed nations there is no separation within the economic system between the necessities of life and the necessities of prestige and power; and that the former can be manipulated in the interest of the latter. Although in some tribal societies manipulation of the economic system is indeed a way to power and prestige, the *necessities of existence* are rarely the object of manipulation.[2] For example, in Alor, a tiny island in the Dutch East Indies, the natives are driven by the quest for economic honour, but this honour is obtained through the accumulation of purely ceremonial objects called *mokos*, and nobody can control garden produce or building materials, which are the mainstay of existence. In this way power and prestige are accessible but the necessities of life are protected. Where they can be manipulated for the sake of power, profit and prestige, the population is vulnerable indeed, for then the things they need are subject to the uncontrolled interplay of strivings that are irrelevant to physical existence.

The Economics of Fear

At last it is necessary to look briefly at vulnerability to foreign powers. It is already a commonplace of American economic history that the balance-wheel in the American economy and the force that has pushed it to unprecedented heights of national opulence, is war production. Thus in a curious way, unique in world history, we prosper by our feelings of vulnerability, because fear of a foreign enemy is converted into well-being by the alchemy of our economic system. Hence we literally grow fat with fear; and in a country presumably trembling from fear of destruction, where people should grow gaunt with terror, reducing diets are among the fastest selling items. We have made of our fear a Roman holiday.

Yet it is well-known that fear is a Mephistopheles that exacts

2. See R. F. Barton, *Ifugao Law*, University of California Publications in Archeology and Ethnology, Vol. XV, for the contrary situation.

extreme payment for benefits and that the benefits are illusions. So that the binding of our economy by obsession with communism has made the economy inflexible in response to other needs, and through embargoes has cut us off from trade with nearly half the world.

Because of manifold fears inherent in our economy and international relations – because we feel so vulnerable at home and abroad – an American political campaign readily becomes a forest of ambiguities nurtured on the soil of public fear, as each party finds a way to reach us through our feelings of vulnerability; and we fly from one to the other not so much because one has a better policy than the other but because one is less frightening than the other. As far as the average voter is concerned it is no longer possible for him to make a fruitful distinction between what is chosen because it makes sense and what is chosen because the alternative is frightful. In our culture they both mean the same thing to the average person.

Bringing Men to Heel

While social scientists consider protection a requisite of society, it is also essential that society makes men vulnerable, for if a man is invulnerable society cannot reach him; and if society produces men who cannot be reached it cannot endure. Thus society will protect us only if we consent to being relatively defenceless. To the end that man can be injured and thus brought to heel, an array of frightful devices has been created so that men will be meek and mild, even to being meek and mild in order to be violent and terrible, like the soldier who obeys orders to kill. From all this it follows that in order for society to survive it must create a vulnerable character structure in its members. The combination of factors that make us thus vulnerable I call the *vulnerability system*.

Where is man vulnerable and how is his vulnerability accomplished? To begin with, we must have a clear idea of the areas of existence in which man is exposed to injury. First there is his reputation – his good name. Since a person protects it by learning the norms of his social class and never deviating, reputation depends on careful study of norms and obedience to them, however one may despise them. Of course it is always better if one believes in them, and this is the effortless way of maintaining a good reputation, of being socially invulnerable. But maintaining a good reputation must involve also a certain amount of concealment – of hiding one's deviations. Since deviation can be in thought as well as in action, invulnerability of reputation involves learning how to conceal deviant thoughts. Hence the person with an invulnerable reputation knows how to conceal his socially unacceptable thoughts – if he ever has any. Of course, the best way to handle deviant thoughts is NOT to have any. This requires either looking away quickly from the socially unpleasant; or, better still, never looking at anything closely.

How does society make people excruciatingly sensitive to the possibilities of and dangers in losing reputation and how does society make one sensitive to one's vulnerability? It is done through placing reputation – the social person – in the centre of consideration and making reputation destiny; by degrading the *inner* self to second, third, or merely adventitious place, and making the social façade supreme, so that at every step the self will be sacrificed to the façade.

How is this manoeuvre accomplished? Surely it can be accomplished best through acquiescence and through disregarding and even punishing the emerging self. It is not so much, however, that the child is punished for asserting his selfhood, but that the thrusting upward of the self is not even seen; what is seen by the parent is largely what is relevant to social requirements; what contributes to a good name; what makes one socially invulnerable. In this way the spirit is pruned, largely insensibly, of everything that is not socially acceptable and self becomes identical with reputation. This need not be so, for it is possible for a person to lose his good name and yet accomplish good things in the name of his self. Great reformers and creators have often done this.

An important function of the feeling of vulnerability is to make us dependent. As small children we are overwhelmed by our vulnerability and so lean on parents, who have in this way become exalted in our eyes. Thus another function of vulnerability is to enlarge the image of those who could harm us and those who protect us. Society is built on a foundation of inflated images derived from vulnerability and upheld by the feeling that what is important are the norms and not our selves.

While in our culture dependence on parents is necessary and very real in childhood, a function of the inflated parental image is to project the child's feeling of vulnerability far beyond the boundaries of realism – in order that society itself may be protected. Thus behind every inflated authority image lies society's fear that it is vulnerable. Behind every inflated image lies society's determination to cancel independence.

The child's vulnerability is sustained and intensified by the elementary school, where he is at the teacher's mercy. The teacher, clearly through no fault of her own, is the agent of vulnerability; and she transmits the sense of it to the child through two weapons thrust into her hands, sometimes against her will – discipline and the power to fail the child. Before these absolute weapons the child is even more vulnerable than with his parents; for with his parents the agony of vulnerability is allayed in part by love, and he can, within limits, fight back. In school, however, this usually is not the case, for in the first place, in the contemporary overcrowded classroom fighting back is a negation of necessary order and routine, and fear of failure is the pulse of school life. Remove the fear of failure, and education in America would stop. Yet we cannot blame the feeling of vulnerability on fear of failure, for after all, without fear of failure, nobody would try for success, and without striving for success there could be no contemporary culture. Thus another characteristic of vulnerability – its roots in the idea of success.

Fear of failure does not begin in school, for in our culture even the basic biological functions of early childhood are amalgamated with the ideas of success and failure. Moving his bowels at the right time and in the right place is a great success for a young child; while losing control and doing it on the living-room rug is a failure, a source of shame and disgrace. Even taking the right amount of milk from the bottle, and eating all one's spinach before getting dessert are successes while leaving food on one's plate, or eating sloppily so that milk dribbles on one's shirt may be considered failures. Thus a baby is already psychologically vulnerable at the mouth and bowel, and thus in our culture fear of failure is built right into the biological functions. In this way the soul is prepared for the intensified fear of failure instilled all through school, including college and graduate school.

Related to such fears is the college student's query of 'Will I make it?', and for many college is a four-year opium sleep in which the answer to the question is postponed, while the student commits himself to the pleasures of a co-educational school as a courting pavilion, while at the same time trying to make himself invulnerable to the dangers of the socio-economic system. And this is the paradox – that, even as the undergraduate is presumably arming, he gives himself up to pleasure in order to forget the enemy.

Thus fear of failure is the dark aspect of the hope and striving for success. For most of us, our abilities, our good looks and our social techniques – our pleasant, public-relations hellos, our ability to laugh at anybody's jokes, our capacity to hold conventional opinions and to never value or fight for any position in an argument too much – never seem quite adequate to ward off all the chances of failure. If a young person is successful in competition for one grade, one scholarship, one boy or girl or one position today, can he be sure of being successful next time? In our culture a person's armour of personal capabilities is never predictably adequate; so that as with the stock market and the gross national product, one can never be sure that if one's capabilities are high today they will not decline tomorrow.

From this long training in feeling vulnerable the graduate student enters the academic world with a greater concern with reputation than with self, and a great fear of failure. Under these conditions he is likely to be a failure to his self, and at this point the *coup de grâce* is often administered to it.

Vulnerability of the Self

The inner self is the part of us that is most vulnerable. Almost as vulnerable is the mind; but the course of civilization has shown that, although we have mastered techniques for sealing off the mind by educating children to be stupid, people safely sealed off from dangerous ideas may still be exceedingly vulnerable to attacks on the self from within.

Attacks on the self begin early but I shall skip the earliest years in the interest of discussing *the expendable self*. In a society oriented towards success, and where fear of failure is thus the commonest nightmare, people have to find ways of being successful and avoiding failure that go far beyond their material assets and skills. The commonest way of becoming successful is by selling one's *self* into slavery to the success pirates. In order to get ahead we give in, say yes when we mean no, praise a book in a review when we think it no good, are nice to a person we detest, or merely keep silent. But the self that is sold in this way gives us no rest, returning to torment us in our dreams; and thus we become vulnerable from within, held in torment by the self we deemed expendable. The dreams in which we become dirty arise from the self to whom we have done dirt.

Another important source of inner vulnerability is job choice, for since most of us do the job we think we have to do, rather than the job we want to do, because we want to marry a certain girl, or please our parents, or have a fancy living standard; or because we don't think we have the ability to do what we want to do, or because we don't have the money to get on with what we want to do, we give up our job dreams and settle down and do what is expedient. But this is just what the inner self never accepts, for regardless of the external reason for giving up, the inner self never forgives. When we deliberately thrust aside our very own job aspirations the inner self sits in judgement on us like a court. A court of law is not interested that one stole because he was hungry or that one killed because he was humiliated; it merely punishes because one has committed the crime. The inner self is in no way different; it is a life-long jury sitting in narrow judgement on us; and if we ignore our true aspirations it poisons life with guilt.

By the time we reach adolescence, giving in, giving up, and a menagerie of impulses that are socially unacceptable have made us so afraid of our inner selves that we seal others off from it. Our motto then becomes, 'Nobody, and this includes myself, will ever know what I am really like', and against this fear of being discovered we erect the wall Freud called 'resistance'. But though resistance prevents discovery it also is a prison, for if people cannot reach us neither can we reach them, and they are always distant from us. So we become façades to one another, living always with the illusions created by the façades. Thus the penalty for invulnerability from discovery is isolation and illusion.

While man in the West is thus a vulnerable creature, who has generated the very instruments that attack him, some are more vulnerable than others, for inner as well as for outer reasons. We all know that the poor are more vulnerable to the economic system than the rich. It is a platitude that money gives the rich man access where the door is shut against the poor. But there is another factor that defends some better than it does others, and that is hope. Having hope, I can confront the future and hope to triumph over the past, but deprived of hope anxiety assaults me. If somebody has made me into dirt, and I have no hope, doubts assail me as to whether I can ever become anything. If I am in despair with loneliness and lovelessness I will die if I lose hope. In the past religion has been a defence against despair, giving man hope, defending him somewhat against doubts, guilt and loneliness, but man in our culture has turned from religion precisely in proportion as western culture, along with its immense productive capability, has acquired the capacity to proliferate occasions for despair that pierces the protective illusions of religion. Outstanding among these have been economic disaster and modern war.

The paradox of man-in-the-West is that the more he has advanced technically the greater his capacity for generating despair; until he has finally made despair itself a factor in production, building armaments, developing advertising, and in general exploiting the feeling of vulnerability itself to keep his system going.

Vulnerability in the Educational System

An Example. In the world outside the university many institutions ensure that the sense of vulnerability will never be lost. Every teacher in a public-school system, for example, knows that if he asserts his self the probabilities of getting a raise or even keeping his job become reduced. But behind the principal who makes this clear to him is a superintendent who can punish the principal, and behind the superintendent is a board of education, while behind *them* is a state department of education ready to punish them all. Behind the state department are the people. Now the circle is complete, for the people, after all, are interested largely in preserving their good name; since many among them have given up self-striving, why should they allow it to anybody else? Furthermore they are frightened about what might happen to their non-conforming children.

It is now time to ask, 'How shall a person who wishes to

assert his *self* in the school system become invulnerable or at least reduce his vulnerability?' By *self*-assertion I do not necessarily mean yelling at the principal, although it is rarely that assertion of one's self does not entail standing up to a superior. By assertion of the self I mean doing and saying what is in harmony with a self that is striving for something significant; for something which would be a step in the direction of self-realization; in the direction of something that enables one to say of one's self, 'I have made myself more significant in my own eyes.' It is *this* self, which studies and evaluates remorselessly, that I am talking about. For a teacher, assertion of the self would involve saying what he thinks most enlightening to the students; refusing to use stupid books, or reinterpreting them to make sense; deviating from the embalmed curriculum; and so on. Alone he obviously can do this only within limits – although, when we come to think of it, the country is so starved for teachers now that after a squabble a teacher can often go around the corner to the next school district and get another job; while principals who once never thought twice before letting a teacher go now think a hundred times. On the other hand, going it alone is foolish, not so much because of the teacher's vulnerability but because if his ideas are good other teachers should share and express them; and if the majority of teachers in the same school do, it is difficult to withstand them. If a teacher acts alone and is forced to lie down or quit, the sense of vulnerability is intensified throughout the school system. The sense of vulnerability functions in a school system to frighten the teachers into becoming stupid; and since when they become stupid so do the pupils, we end up with the understanding that vulnerability in the teacher helps educate children to stupidity. In this way society gets what it wants.

The functioning of the vulnerability system is illustrated by the case of Virginia Franklin, a high-school teacher in Paradise, California, as reported in *Life*.

I quote from the article:

The rage in Paradise centres on a high-school teacher named Virginia Franklin. She believes America is served best by training children to make up their own minds. Her social-studies classes, filled with debate, are encouraged to read material of widely divergent points of view, from the liberal to the extremes of the right wing.

Mrs Franklin earned an award from the Freedoms Foundation, but gained the enmity of the local American Legion post and others, including the John Birch Society. She was, of course, accused of being a communist, and one of her students was discovered spying on her in class by means of a tape recorder hidden in a hole carved in a text book. Fortunately Mrs Franklin had the support of the principal, superintendent and a small majority of people who voted in the election for a new member of the school board. Mrs Franklin's supporters won.

This case has many features of the vulnerability system as it operates in our country. It is seen to have its roots in irrational fear and hate and it takes possession of a revered symbol, in this case love of country. But it appropriates the fear symbol *also*, which in this case is communism, for the extreme right considers itself the sole defender of the country. Mrs Franklin would have been vulnerable had she stood alone: but what is most striking is that although the principal, the superintendent and the school board supported her during the outbreak of lunacy, the other teachers did not come forward.

The comment of Dr George Baron of the Institute of Education of the University of London is vital in connection with the case. Writing in *The Teachers College Record*,[3] he says:

The Hell in Paradise case . . . gives to an English reader at first the impression of a closed, insular little society in which all is distrust and suspicion . . .

3. May 1964, pp. 667–70.

There was, it would seem, no structure of accepted authority and custom to which the participants could appeal, no firmly held views on what was the nature of the trust that parent, teacher, and pupil must have in each other and in each other's roles, in the school situation. Moreover . . . neither teacher nor principal was effectively supported by any professional association; *no university appears to have lent its weight to the cause of the teacher's freedom, and no figures of significance in the intellectual and political life of the nation seized on the incident as one to be lifted out of its purely parochial context.* It was left then, for the . . . small community of Paradise to decide unaided issues that have occupied men for centuries. [Italics supplied]

Thus Dr Baron sees to the core: the distrust and suspicion, which spread like cancer; the readiness of hate and fear-motivated organizations to usurp power where no clear authority exists; and the oceanic lack of involvement of the American people in their own vulnerable predicament. This is brought out by Dr Baron's remarks that no professional association, no university – especially professors of education – came forward to be heard on the matter. Like the New Yorkers who watched from behind their blinds while a woman was stabbed to death,[4] they remained uninvolved. As long as Americans are uninvolved in one another each stands alone in his vulnerability. We conclude from this that a consequence of extreme vulnerability, wherein all men stand alone, is to make all men vulnerable; to bring all men to heel. Commenting further Dr Baron says:

This is markedly different from the situation in England – or, indeed, in Europe generally – where the universities, the schools, and the professions together have a coherence that protects them and individual teachers and practitioners from local and other external pressures.

In conclusion he says:

4. Reported in the *New York Times*, 27 March 1964.

Given the place accorded to the local community in school affairs (in the United States), the isolation of the teacher, the seriousness of the heed paid to the views of children and adolescents, the political function ascribed to the school (as a controller of political ideas), and the fear of uncontrolled unusual ideas, other Paradises are inevitable. Teachers and parents who support mildly controversial ideas, *even though they are commonplaces throughout the Western world*, must then live with the fear of being denounced and persecuted.

On the Nature and Causes of Incompetence

Since a consequence of vulnerability is to prevent social change, and since in our culture there is always a strong push for enlightened social change, we conclude that usually the function of the vulnerability system is to prevent enlightenment and the consequent change. Put another way, the function of the vulnerability system is often to guarantee darkness and incompetence. As a matter of fact the people who are in the positions most strategic for social change are usually the most vulnerable. In government an outstanding example of this is the United States Department of Labor, which, though originally established to look after the interests of labour, was quickly deprived of power because of the danger of too great closeness of labour and government. Shorn of real power the Department of Labor became a frozen bureaucracy dedicated largely to collecting statistics and keeping out of trouble with Congress, the Department of State and organized labour itself who came to look upon the Department as largely a do-nothing outfit, uninterested in labour's welfare and under the thumb of Congress and business.

In education the group most strategic for social change is the teachers, and we know that the teachers are a vulnerable group. Fifty years ago labour was in a similar position, and it is only through organizing that it lost its vulnerability. As soon as this happened, however, labour lost interest in social change also. This suggests that although a vulnerable group cannot institute social change, once it has become invulnerable it may lose its interest in social change.

As a group becomes invulnerable, either through organization or through freezing in self-protective attitudes, it also becomes incompetent, because within the cake of protection that freezes around it there are frozen also the skills the group is seeking to protect. Hence teachers don't change, superintendents don't change, and workers do not take the trouble to educate themselves beyond the skills guaranteed to them by their organization. Over the years invulnerability through hiding has become the very factor that has now made educators increasingly vulnerable to the criticism of incompetence.

The Illuminating Case of Descartes

Most of us have learnt in introductory courses in philosophy that Descartes was so afraid of the church that he had to prove many times that God exists; that he withdrew several of his works on hearing of the condemnation of Galileo, and that he insisted on anonymity. Less well known is the probability that Descartes avoided discovering calculus because he was afraid that analysis of infinity would be considered blasphemy. Anyone who knows Descartes's capacities – that he started western philosophy on new pathways, that he is a fundamental source of modern phenomenology, and that he invented analytical geometry – could not doubt, after reading his *Principles*, that he could have discovered calculus had he not been afraid of inquiring into the nature of infinity. Consider the following from Principles XXVI and XXVII:

The heading of Principle XXVI reads as follows:

That we must not try to dispute about the infinite, but just consider that all that in which we find no limits is indefinite, such as the extension of the world, the divisibility of its parts, the number of the stars, etc.

The *Principle* continues:

We will thus never hamper ourselves with disputes about the infinite, since it would be absurd that we who are finite should undertake to decide anything regarding it . . . That is why we do not care to reply to those who demand whether the half of an infinite line is infinite, and whether an infinite number is even or odd and so on . . . And for our part, while we regard things in which, in a certain sense, we observe no limits, we shall not for all that state that they are infinite, but merely hold them to be indefinite. Thus because we cannot imagine an extension so great that we cannot at the same time conceive that there may be one yet greater, we shall say that the magnitude of possible things is indefinite.

Now come the lines that make clear that the calculus was within Descartes's reach:

And because we cannot divide a body into parts which are so small that each part cannot be divided into others yet smaller, we shall consider that the quantity may be divided into parts whose number is indefinite.

Since infinity and the infinitesimal are at the core of the calculus and since Descartes discovered analytical geometry, necessary preliminary to calculus, it is probable he would have discovered calculus too if he had not been afraid. Principle XXVII makes the issue even clearer.
He says:

And we shall name these things indefinite rather than infinite in order to reserve to God alone the name of infinite, first of all because in Him alone we observe no limitation whatever, and because we are quite certain that He can have none. [I change now to the French translation, because the issues are clearer there.][5] As regards other

5. The English translators indicate that Descartes was enthusiastic about the French translation and that he wrote the Preface. See *Philosophical Works of Descartes*; translated into English by Elizabeth S. Haldane and G. R. T. Ross (Cambridge, 1967), Vol. I, p. 202.

things we know that they are not thus absolutely perfect because although we observe in them certain *properties which appear to have no limit,* we yet know that *this proceeds from our lack of understanding and not from their natures.*

So, he says, man must leave the infinite and the infinitesimal unplumbed because they belong to God and are beyond understanding – even though it was clear that Descartes understood them. Thus the sensation of vulnerability prevented Descartes from making a great discovery; and from this we conclude that *behind many intellectual failures lies a failure of nerve.*

The Bureaucratization of Knowledge and the Growth of Incompetence

A bureaucracy is a hierarchically organized institution whose purpose is to carry on certain limited functions. Thus a school system, the army, a university, the government, are all bureaucracies. It is common knowledge, however, that bureaucracies have three functions, rather than one. Although the first is ostensibly to carry out the tasks for which they are established, the definition of roles and the routinization of procedures in bureaucracies brings it about that an important function of the organization becomes that of preventing anything within it from changing. Even small change might make it necessary for the entire organization to change because each part is so interlocked with every other, that to alter any procedure in a bureaucracy without changing the rest is often like trying to increase the height of one wall of a house without modifying its entire configuration. A third function of a bureaucracy is to perpetuate itself. Given the functions of preventing internal change and struggling to survive, bureaucracies tend to devote much of their time to activities that will prevent change. Under these conditions it is difficult to introduce new knowledge into the system. Often only a general convulsion in the total society can compel a bureaucracy to change; and then it will do so only just enough to avoid going out of business. Obviously these are the conditions for incompetence: bureaucracies create the conditions for their own incompetence and hence for their own destruction. World convulsions have caused radical changes in the administration of the executive in our own government; the changes in the Department of Defense have been a response to world crisis; and the entrenched military brass have almost been swept away because they would not change. And so it goes. The feeling of vulnerability always creates efforts at defence but these very efforts only increase vulnerability over the long run because they cause incompetence. The feeling of vulnerability, efforts at defence by freezing the system, increased vulnerability and ultimate destruction if there is no change – this is the universal law of Western Civilization.

Competence for Whom? And for What?

Anybody in our culture who suggested that we did not love our children would be hated; and in harmony with our love of children we want them to have the best education available. Of course, it has to be the best education available for the money we are willing to spend, and we all know that in calculating the amount of money we are able – or rather, are willing – to spend on education, the family standard of living comes first. That is to say, after we have calculated expenditures for food, liquor, entertainment, the kind of clothes that will present us and our children to the world in conformity with our class position, expenditures for fishing tackle, guns, high-fi sets, radios (several in one house), TV (two or three in one house), out-board-motor boats, two cars, $30–$40 dresses for the kid's graduation prom, two or more bathing suits for everybody, a summer vacation, a barbecue pit, a nice house with suitable mortgage and upkeep, hairdoes, mouthwashes, cosmetics, cigarettes, bowling, movies and repairs on the car – I say, after we have calculated all these expenses – not to mention taxes to state and federal governments – we are willing to give our children the best education to be bought with the money that's left over. Obviously not much is, and the extreme difficulty we always have in increasing education budgets is witness to the contradiction between educational goals and the living standard. Thus education, the very phenomenon that made a rising living standard possible, is undermined by it.

Another factor contributing heavily to incompetence in education is war, for since taxes to support it are heavy, we are unwilling to be taxed for other things; that is to say, we are unwilling to pay higher education taxes in the interests of our children. When we add the expenditures for the commitment to a good time and a rising standard of living to expenditures for war, our children get the dirty end of the stick. Let us put it even more clearly: as far as education is concerned, war, a good time and the living standard eat up so much that in their education the kids get the crumbs that fall from the table. Educational crumbs can be only educational incompetence. On the other hand, in a deeper sense, our children get the best education compatible with a society that requires a high level of stupidity in order to exist as it is. A moment's reflection will convince anyone that this is true. For example, if television had a truly well-educated audience and the newspapers and magazines well-educated readers, the economy would collapse because since nobody would then be impressed by the advertising, they would not buy. Adults who had been trained by clear-headed, sharp-brained teachers would be imbued with such clarity of vision that they would not put up with many federal and local policies and they certainly would stop smoking. They might even begin to question the need for a standard of living that has spread wall-to-wall carpeting from here to California and given millions more space and more mobility than they can intelligently use. In the light of these terrifying possibilities the thought of an education in depth and sharpness for everybody can only make a thoughtful person anxious, because an education for stupidity is the only one we can afford right now.

I hope it is understood that no criticism is intended of socially necessary education for stupidity. Having been an educator much of my life I understand that every civilization needs to introduce a reasonable amount of respectable intellectual sabotage into its educational system lest the young get out of hand and challenge or scorn tradition and accepted canons of truth.

Education and War

If we look at education and the war from the standpoint of vulnerability, we see that in many ways education in this country today is hostage to our fear of communism; and revisions in the courses in maths and science are not going to help the child much; they are just going to make him better for the war machine and for the changing character of American industry, which each day becomes more and more dependent on the sciences. Revision of the teaching of science and math will not help the child much because we are not improving his skills in math and science in the interest of his inner self but in the interest of war and industry. Furthermore, the overwhelming majority of girls will have no use for it and college students show a declining interest in the sciences. The history of American education in the last hundred years shows that education has not considered the child's interest but that of industry; and I am not yet convinced that what is good for General Motors is good for our children. Even less am I convinced that what is good for Missile Dynamics is good for our children, or what is good for the Pentagon is good for them. Meanwhile the educational system, pressed by one world movement or local interest after the other, successively breeds one form of incompetence after the other. Each world hysteria generates a powerful group that sees itself as prophet of the system, and the system yields to it. It is yield or die, because for the moment they hold overwhelming power.

It thus becomes clear that love of our children is, at best, qualified by our love of fun and the high-rising living standard, and that adults do not love their children so much that they are willing to lower their living standard and give up some fun in the interest of raising the level of education to what is more in conformity with the possibilities of the richest and one of the most democratic countries in the world. It is also clear that *although we love our own children it is not so clear that others – like industry or the Pentagon – love them in the same way and for the same reasons.*

Summary and Conclusions

I have spoken of the vulnerability – the susceptibility to destruction and defeat – of man in our culture. In answer to the questions, 'What makes man vulnerable and why do people feel vulnerable', I sought the answer first in the desperate uncertainty of our economic system, which today flies in the face of all economic theory by relying heavily on war production: so that, against the entire experience of mankind, we are anxious about what warlessness might do to us. In considering the general instability of our type of economic system, I pointed out that it demands consumption to the degree that department stores have become the Louvres and the Museums of Natural History and Art of our culture; to the degree that a famous book on advertising speaks, as might a book on biology, of the evolution of toothpaste, beer, shaving cream and so on.

My primary purpose in discussing the vulnerability of our social and economic systems was to provide a background for understanding our feelings of inner vulnerability – primarily the feeling that compels us to sell our selves down the river to the pirates of success.

I have tried to show how disrespect for our very selves seals us off from others and therefore leaves us with a sense of loneliness and isolation. I pointed out that in order for society to continue it has to make us vulnerable – it has to create in us a vulnerable character structure, for did we not feel vulnerable society would have no way of making us toe the mark. I discussed Descartes because I wanted to show how what attacks all of us in the scholarly world – fear of punishment for making the very discoveries which are the goal and glory of our calling – prevented Descartes from discovering the calculus. Anyone who reads history and the social sciences critically learns that behind many intellectual failures is indeed a failure of nerve. The books we are compelled to give our students – largely because there are no better ones – are often boring and irritating, not because their authors lack brains but because they lack courage.

Thus it turns out that incompetence in education is in large part a consequence of fear – fear of one another and fear of communism, and the case of Mrs Franklin is merely an extreme and overt expression of the widespread but covert process of sabotage that plagues the educational system and helps make our children stupid. But the incompetence of the educational system is merely one form of bureaucratic incompetence, and all bureaucracies become incompetent because of fear.

The moral of all this is that we must know our strength. Nobody is invulnerable but nobody is as weak as he thinks he is either. Let everyone, instead of saying to himself, 'I am afraid', say instead, 'I may be stronger than I think.'

6. Values: Guilt, Suffering, and Consequences*

It is characteristic of any culture that the ordinary person does not define the central values that guide his conduct, even though they press him inexorably in the direction of one kind of behaviour and interdict others. The arguments that engage philosophers do not concern him, even though in the long run they do affect him. The effect is not in terms of the definition or redefinition of his conduct, but rather in terms of his *reinforcement*: fundamentally no philosopher is outside his culture – he can merely formulate predominant attitudes and ideas and reintroduce them into the schools, strengthened by the prestige and the arrogance of the academic position.

The Inner Colloquy

In an effort to depict the characteristic value anxiety through which an ordinary citizen passes I have prepared the following models of inner colloquies.

Honesty:

What is good? Honesty is good.
What do I practise? I practise a mixture of honesty and dishonesty.
How do I feel about it? I feel guilty for my dishonesty and not proud
    of my honesty. Perhaps I practise honesty only when I must and

* Reprinted from the *School Review*, Vol. LXXI, No 4, 1963.

dishonesty when I can . . . who knows? I do the best I can . . . yes, I guess I do. Or do I?

How is the world? The world is largely dishonest. But on second thought there are some honest people. Or are there? There are plenty of people who are at least as dishonest as I am, *that's* for sure; and a lot who are worse; for example . . . The most dishonest people generally turn out to be those who criticize others for dishonesty, for example . . .

What do I want for my children? I want them to succeed . . . I mean, I want them to be honest within the possibilities offered them by the need to succeed. I want people to be honest with *them*.

Courage:

What is good? Courage is good.

What do I do? Sometimes I'm courageous; mostly I'm afraid.

How do I feel about it? I feel guilty, but I do the best I can . . . or do I? I am courageous when I have nothing to lose – but is this courage? On the other hand, who is unafraid?

How is the world? The world is made up of powerful people, for whom courage therefore comes easy, because they are strong; and wishy-washy people, who are afraid because they are weak, or at least they think they are weak. There are also 'those who know on which side their bread is buttered'. Powerful people generally wipe their feet on the weak, and the weak are without courage because they are weak.

What do I want for my children? I want my children to be courageous, but I want them also to get on in the world.

Protection:

What is good? It is good to protect others.

What do I do? I protect myself; and I protect others when it will not hurt me.

How do I feel about it? Sometimes I am about to protect somebody and fear comes icily upon me, so I stop. I feel guilty about this. But am I my brother's keeper? Who will protect *me* when I expose myself to danger? Protecting others seems always to endanger me, whether I am trying to sell Coca-Cola (which is bad for her teeth) to little Alice Jones or saving her from being hit by a car. If I don't sell the Coke, I lose my job; and if I slip or move too slowly the car will hit me. I try very hard to forget about protection.

How is the world? Most people care only about themselves.

What do I want for my children? I want the world to protect my children, and I want my children to succeed. After all, they have to look out for themselves.

Some Derivative Truisms and Logical Derivatives

1. Nobody can follow 'the good'.
2. People feel guilty in the presence of 'the good'.
3. The most comfortable culture must be one without goodness.
4. The most comfortable culture is based on expediency and not on values.
5. The function of values is to generate guilt.
6. The function of guilt is to generate values.
7. Parents do not want their children to adhere to 'the good', but they want the world to practise 'the good' with respect to their children.
8. Parents and teachers should teach children expediency.
9. But then people will treat them as is expedient.
10. It is better to teach children to practise 'the good'.
11. It is better to teach children how to practise artful chicanery.
12. Courage is a virtue suited only to courageous people.
13. It is easier to be expedient than courageous; hence courage should be abandoned.
14. One cannot abandon courage, because that is cowardly and unethical.
15. People can be happy only in a secure world, but to protect others may imperil one's self.
16. To protect only one's self is expedient, but carelessness with regard to the perils of others deprives one of social protection; therefore, protect others. However, this can be done only with reservation.

17. Let us give heed then to preparing a list of reservations.
18. This is all nonsense. Let us teach values pure and simple.
19. But this is not the way the world runs.
20. To hell with the world.
21. You send the world to hell and it will crucify *you*!

I have formulated as inner colloquies the value paradoxes that have confronted our cultural tradition for several millenniums, because in our cultural tradition all value debates become inner debates, even though they may not have originated that way. In our cultural tradition value considerations, or rather value dilemmas, have been agonizing inner debates from which man has tried to escape by talk, by flight from the problem, or by extrication through use of all the inner devices available to him.

The inner colloquies I have presented suggest that contemporary man is marooned in his value paradoxes. He is as if on an island from which there is no escape except in a boat of leaky excuses. When one studies the families of psychotic children, one perceives that for their parents values are merely a trap,[1] not a guide to a full life; and it is a symptom of the social pathology of our time, as the inner colloquies suggest, that values are for many people a deadfall rather than a guide to life. This is the meaning of my models.

I wish to stress the importance of the inner colloquy, for, in spite of its contradictions, the mere existence of the inner conversation proves that we are still not entirely lost. I stress the inner colloquy also because it stems from the contradiction between what Spinoza called 'eternity' and the 'world'. And I stress the inner colloquy also because its real significance to us and its validity can be measured by the anguish it causes and by our desire to talk, run, rationalize, or wring our hands because of it. If we feel moved to do none of these things, it indicates that we have moved from values, morality and ethics to mere calculation.

1. This problem is discussed in my *Culture against Man*, Chapter 9.

Let us pass now from the problem of the inner colloquy to the problem of the components of an ethical system.

Protection

A decent human society – one in which promises are kept with reasonable regularity; where people keep their word much more often than they break it; where they tell the truth much more often than they lie; where a person presents himself to you as he is, not as he wishes to conceal himself from you; where goals are the manifest intentions of people rather than the hidden ones; where sorcery and nightmares are rare, and emotional illness disproportionately small in relation to the entire population – is bound to be a society in which protection of the other person forms the kernel of ethical considerations. The underlying idea in the value *honesty* is protection of the other person. Whether it be the return of the proper change to a customer, the refusal to sell defective merchandise or to rig prices, or letting your secretary know at once that you intend to discharge her instead of waiting until you have another one lined up, the central problem is protection of the other person. To be honest with So-and-so means merely that you treat him in such a way – by telling him the truth, for example, when it might be to your advantage to lie – that he is protected from the consequences of an untruth. The concept of protection – rather than truth or honesty – enables us to understand that at times it is wrong to tell the truth because the truth sometimes does not protect but destroys. It is very likely that virtue itself can be reduced to solicitude for other people. Since it is clear that the anchorage of any ethical system must be in the other person, let us consider the problem of anchorage.

Anchorage of the System

It is natural that a reasonable man would consider a good moral system one in which both parties in a situation involving their interests emerged gainers. But it must be apparent to any reasonable man also that there are many situations in which not everybody can gain from the immediate transaction, or even over the long run – at least, not gain in terms of any common coin, such as money, a rise in status, or more comfortable living accommodations. In such cases somebody must lose, and it is central to my conception of morality, as well as to that of many before me, that one must learn to lose in the interest of enhancing the well-being of another person. At any rate, no ethical system can really be one unless it is *anchored in – not merely considers* – the other person. Value systems that are worthy of the name must *start* with postulating the well-being of the other person or persons or nations or the world as a necessary beginning of the ethical chain of reasoning.

This does not mean that the actor (or Ego) can never think of himself, for such self-destructive conduct is possible only for saints. Even mothers cannot think only of their children, for this might soon so impair their efficiency as mothers that the welfare of the family would be endangered.

Suffering

This brings us to the problem of suffering as inherent in any consideration of ethics. The Old Testament adage, 'Do not do unto others what you would not have them do unto you', does not quite state the nature of the human condition in our culture, for it omits the obvious truth that in many human transactions with good will on both sides somebody is bound to suffer. The great dilemma in *American* thinking about ethics is that many cannot bear the idea of depriving themselves, and this problem is especially acute today, where in an affluent society, in what is still the most powerful economy in the world and in which so many natural (extra-human) forces have been brought under control, it is difficult, and even economically inappropriate, to bear the pain of deprivation. The American is a rambunctious, driving, expanding, gaining, self-indulgent, spend-thrift creature to whom deprivation is horrifying; and to confront the idea that a decent society requires the embracing of deprivation and pain as a normal and regular component in living together is difficult for him.

In considering the relevance of self-deprivation and even suffering to an ethical system, we thus face the fact that the conception is antagonistic to our contemporary culture. Yet the dilemma is that if we leave this element out of ethical decisions we get either a pleasure system or one based on games theory. Neither of these is an ethical system; for, as I have said, the central factor in an ethical system for man in our culture must be protection of others. Without depriving one's self, protection of others can rarely occur.

Suffering, however, cannot be an end in itself for ordinary mortals; nor can protection be an end in itself. As I suggested earlier, the mother who exhausts herself in the interests of her child may do no good over the long run. It is the essence of the human condition that man must balance his solicitude for others against his own need for survival *in the interest of the other person*. At the same time also, it would be piously pretentious to insist that man not think of himself in a selfish way also.

The problem of the relevance of suffering to an ethical system, meanwhile, requires more intricate and imaginative treatment than I can give it here – or, perhaps, anywhere. However, a prime consideration is that one often does not stand to suffer as much as one thinks; and another is that often unexpected rewards accrue to a person who renounces his own gain. Important also is the deep and solemn sense of self-realization that comes upon one when one has deprived oneself or even suffered in the interest of enhancing the life of another.

If one looks at the question, 'What do I want for my children?' in the inner colloquy, he will see that the ordinary citizen does not want the world to hurt his child. If people want the world to be honest with their children; if they want the world not to injure their children when they are courageous; and if parents want the world to protect their children, it follows that they cannot make demands on the world that are different from the ones they make on themselves. I cannot ask the world to protect my children and to be honest with them, and then turn around and do the opposite. When people do this, they will get the kind of world they deserve. Nor can one ask the world to be honest, courageous, and protective to one's children and not expect that this will cause the world pain. I cannot expect the department store to refuse to sell shoddy merchandise to my child (and thus hurt itself) while I sell shoddy merchandise myself. Yet it is expected.

What many ask from the world is that it should protect their children while they protect themselves.

This brings us to the problem of the world.

Values Versus 'The World'

It is obvious to everybody that ethical and value ideas tend to collide with what we call 'the world'; that is, the everyday life of wealth- and status-striving, where people knock each other down. A very good but true story, told by our Professor Levi at Washington University in St Louis, illustrates the point. A certain famous professor emeritus of philosophy, whom we shall call Jones, was hard of hearing and used an old-fashioned ear-trumpet. One day a young colleague brought to him a certain Professor Smith and introduced him as 'Professor Smith, professor of business ethics'. Jones responded, 'How do you do, Mr Smith', but he turned to his young colleague and asked,

'What did you say he taught?' 'Business ethics,' shouted the colleague, 'What did you say?' said Jones. 'Business ethics,' bellowed the colleague. 'Well, don't bother,' said Jones, 'there's no use repeating it again, because it always sounds as if you were saying "business *ethics*".' Thus there is no point in trying to reconcile values with 'the world', for the world is a jungle, riddled by competition and its consequent and necessary chicanery and distrust. The world is prevented from becoming a complete jungle by law, particularly the laws of contract; by the stability of the currency; and by the anger of the loss of customers.

Systems of relations based on enlightened self-interest are book-keeping systems. One does not apply ethical principles to one's relationship with a pistol pointed at one's head, but rather thinks of one's enlightened self-interest. One should not confuse the so-called business ethics based on the laws of contract, the stability of the currency, and the retention of the market – a satisfied market – with moral principles that govern the relations between human beings. They may resemble each other, but the similarity is purely coincidental and largely illusory. Between human beings one activates the ideas of protection and suffering because one feels it is human to enhance the well-being of another person. But in the market, wherever protection of another enters, it does so in order to *protect one's self*; it is one's market that is involved. In the market the anchorage of the value is always in the *self*; the anchorage in human relations is always in the *other*. This brings us to the difficult problem of the relation between values and the consequences of action.

The Problem of Consequences

In my 'A Cross-Cultural Outline of Education' I examined the problem of unanticipated consequences in its relation to elementary-school programmes, and I said that for the children the problem of consequences of a game, like spelling baseball, for example, could be solved only by taking an inventory of all the possible consequences of the game *after it was over*.[2] Fundamentally, I argued, there can be no theory of 'unanticipated consequences' – as the sociologists call it – because we are usually not able to anticipate consequences in the presence of complex variables. Knowledge of consequences can be based only on inventories of events that have transpired as consequences of regularly repeated actions. That being the case, *un*anticipated consequences can be *anticipated*, and the need for a theory to handle the problem fades away.

In most human events, however, we cannot take inventories, and, since we are not gifted with the insights of gods, we have to guess at consequences. For this purpose we have on the national level professional guessing organizations like the Rand Corporation, and other non-profit corporations, to which the government farms out its guessing problems; and we have produced guessing geniuses like Herman Kahn, who guess, for example, what the chances are of nuclear war with the Russians, how many tens of millions of dead there would be under different conditions, how many cities would be destroyed on both sides of the Atlantic under different conditions, the feasibility of constructing a Doomsday Machine triggered to blow up the world under certain conditions, and so on. Thus various assumptions are made about certain combinations of variables in the nuclear tension, the assumptions are fed to a computer, and a great range of answers is given by the machine. Such a procedure helped produce Kahn's famous book, *On Thermonuclear War*, and also Secretary McNamara's recent ill-fated decision (based on one of Kahn's guesses) to propose to the Russians that we make a gentleman's agreement (an interesting American 'ethical' fantasy) to bomb military targets only. This proposal drew the Russian reply that in thermonuclear war the distinction between military and non-military targets cannot be made because of the size of the blast damage, the necessary

2. *Current Anthropology*, July 1960.

inaccuracy of controls under wartime conditions, and because bombs have no brains and cannot make fine distinctions.

This raises the fundamental problem of the relation between perception and consequences in all value decisions. It will be observed that the Rand computers are programmed for the American mind and not for the Russian. A computer is a machine programmed *to think in the matrix of a particular culture*, and, unless an American guesser is terribly clever, he will instruct the machine to think like an American. Similarly Russian computers will think like Russians, French computers like Frenchmen, etc.

Thus, as I enter into the calculation of the consequences of any act of mine for me and another person, I must take into account not only the large number of variables and the enormously ramifying consequences of all action, but also the nature of the other's *programming*: what he *expects* and how he *perceives* the outcome of action. Thus although I may see the virtue of giving a low mark to a poor student because it may be a spur of action – as a challenge that will urge the student to reform – he may not see it that way at all. It is extremely difficult to develop an ethical theory, based on a calculation of the outcome of an action for both myself *and* the other person, because he may perceive the same outcome differently. The problem becomes even more complex when we take account not of two people only but of groups and nations. Once I rule *myself* out of the calculation, however, and decide to undergo some suffering, once I decide that my central concern is protection of the other person, the problem is simpler—the less I worry about myself, the more I am willing to accept suffering as a natural part of living – I have less need for a computer.

The Value of Conscience

Much of the contemporary problem of values derives from that annoying mechanism, conscience. Conscience is what wrings our hearts and disturbs our dreams when the inner colloquy speaks in voices of complaint. Conscience creates guilt, which, although one of the most powerful instruments of social control ever invented, causes inner malaise and is therefore going out of style. Along with the ethic of suffering, guilt is becoming obsolete; and it is the function of all model 1962 ethical systems to take the guilt out of life. If, however, we remove the guilt from ethics, we remove not one, but several important – and pivotal – feelings. The components of guilt are the following:

1. The desire to conceal
2. The feeling that the person wronged did not deserve what we did to him
3. The desire to make restitution
4. The feeling of being debased in our own eyes
5. The feeling of being debased in the eyes of society or of some significant figure in our lives
6. A generalized anxiety, including fear of punishment
7. The feeling of having violated some ideal
8. A nagging inner reproach

It is obvious that we cannot remove guilt from an ethical system without endangering decent human society, for the abolition of guilt removes the mechanism of self-criticism and the inner need to make restitution for a wrong, and it undermines the capacity to entertain an ideal.

Meanwhile the ethical termites are loose among us gnawing away at the pillars of guilt – and they are probably succeeding. And meanwhile, also, guilt is the last bastion between ethics and expediency. *Where guilt is not, there shall expediency be.*

While guilt is an unpleasant emotion, which, while securing the foundations of a decent society, also causes great inner malaise, it is also an important condition of love, for if one is incapable of guilt one cannot love. The reason is simple: the essence of human love is protection of the beloved and the capacity to suffer for him. Take away guilt therefore, and you remove the imperative to protect and to suffer for another. Under such conditions love is impossible.

Ethics and Ideals

It has been impossible for people reared during the several millenniums of our culture to entertain an ethical system without referring it to an ideal, whether it be the state or God. Since, on the other hand, it is a commonplace that it is becoming increasingly difficult for modern man to entertain any ideals whatsoever, it follows that he can have no ethical system and no values. Yet this condition is impossible for him to confront; for even the most calculating (non-criminal) among us tremble at the thought that *everybody else* should be equally so. What then shall modern man take as an ideal? Or let us put it this way: since ideals are spurs to action and to ethical conduct, what shall be the spur to ethical conduct in modern man? What shall be the pivot of values in the ordinary, the average citizen? *Let it be his own loneliness and misery.* Let him in his isolation from his fellow man reach out with feelings of solicitude but also with the expectation of suffering.

Conclusion

I have attempted to review some of the problems of values as they have occurred to me. Fundamentally I know little of value theory, so I speak only as an ordinary citizen. I have expressed the conviction that the calculation of the probabilities for a mutually advantageous outcome in any value-charged human encounter too quickly becomes a game in which self-interest must predominate, so that one scarcely knows whether one is dealing with a value system or a pragmatic code of expediency dominated by the theory of games. I have urged, on the other hand, that the fundamental component in a value system for man in our culture must be protection of the other person and that such a component is inconceivable without a willingness to suffer pain and deprivation. I have also urged that man in our culture cannot escape from his conscience if he wants to have a decent society; and that without conscience and guilt love itself is impossible. And without love there is no point to the world.

7. Sham*

In *The Devil and the Good Lord* Sartre says that it is impossible to do good and in *No Exit* he tells us that hell is people. In *Tiny Alice* Albee says that whoever does not learn to accept sham as reality deserves to be shot; de Sade argues that only evil succeeds and that virtue is ridiculous and will end up corrupted. Heidegger says that the way to Being is authenticity but that the way to authenticity is through our heritage, which he never defines. Kierkegaard believes that only supine resignation, aided by striving, is the way to God. President Johnson tells us that war is peace, Martin Luther King pats the Illinois National Guard on the back for their politeness while Hubert Humphrey suggests the appropriateness of Negro revolt. The officers of a famous university issue engraved invitations to a 'reception opening the Conference on Poverty in America'; and those who direct anti-poverty programmes are the upper-middle class, who are not in want. It is clear that our civilization is a tissue of contradictions and lies; and that therefore the main problem for psychiatry is not to cure mental illness but to define sanity and account for its occurrence.

I shall devote my remarks to Albee's argument that whoever cannot believe that sham is reality deserves to be shot, because

*Prepared for the Conference on Society and Psychosis, the Hahnemann Medical College, October 1966. Reprinted from the *North American Review*, Vol. 252/3, 1967, pp. 6–8.

I consider this the fundamental intellectual problem of Man-in-the-West. It is obvious that Albee is right, and that is why practically nobody understands his play and why it did not last on Broadway. For we all live every day by sham, anyone who fights against it, makes life unbearable. In schizophrenogenic families sham and confusion infest every aspect of life, so that the people in it draw a crooked breath, so to speak.

Though I was probably very much a sham most of my life, without knowing it – in other words, perfectly socialized to the corrupt system – I seem to have become actively aware of it in others – though still not in myself – through the following incident. I once needed a certain book, rather costly and hard to find. I was directed to a man who had a copy, and when I asked him over the phone whether I might borrow it, he said yes. I came to his house, sat down in his living-room and he went and got the book. He came back, a smile of satanic inner delight on his face, and plumped the book, a rather heavy affair, down in my lap with both hands, while he stood by, a gleam of infinite self-appreciation in his eyes. It was clear from his expression and from the force with which he placed the book in my lap that he did not want me to have it; but it was also clear, from the intense expression of auto-preening on his face, that he enjoyed watching me go through the process of sorting out what he thought were my mixed feelings about the book; for he knew that he had given it to me and withheld it both at the same time. The binding and illustrations were magnificent. Quite apart from the fact that he clearly did not want me to have it, but did not wish to say so directly – possibly because he could not deprive himself of the pleasure of making me uncomfortable, possibly because he shrank from saying no directly, when someone close to him had suggested him – was the fact that the book was so obviously expensive I would not dare borrow it. This, my first clear recollection of the power of sham, gave me insight into a pathogenic process also, for I derived from this encounter the hypothesis that this kind of person may give and withhold both at the same time. A number of years later, when, having torn the veil of sham off a certain psychiatric hospital where I had been employed and therefore was in the market for a job – shot out of a job, so to speak – a letter of inquiry sent to another person, was, unknown to me, given to this man (the man with the book), and his reply was so meaningless I came to a second conclusion, that this kind of person communicates and says nothing, both at the same time. Naturally I did not reply.

These kinds of shams have complex motivations, and the motivational complex behind them fluctuates from action to action, somewhat as follows: consider the following psychic states: depression; hostility; 'realistic' factors, such as the book that is much too expensive to replace; anxiety; feeling of helplessness; confusion; desire to exploit; lack of confidence in being believed; need to maintain appearances. From this partial list of the variety of psychic states that might result in sham, we can perceive that any particular sham can be caused by several factors; that any sham can be the expression of one or more psychic states at the same time. Thus, for example, President Johnson's inability to make clear the Administration's reasons for being in Vietnam may be made up of confusion, the desire to exploit, lack of confidence in being believed and a need to maintain appearances; while his reasons for not being frank about not giving up on NATO may perhaps be referred to 'realistic' factors, a feeling of helplessness, confusion and a need to maintain appearances. These are hypotheses only, meant to illustrate the argument. As for the book, it was perhaps withheld because it was too expensive to replace (a realistic factor); but the sham itself was derived probably from hostility, a feeling of helplessness and also probably from the owner's feeling that he would not be believed if he gave me the right reason and from his need to maintain appearances before me and before the person who suggested his book. The net perplexity was worked out in his taking pleasure in punishing me, by saying yes and no both at once. Thus the pleasure was in part a reflex of his own helplessness. In much of sham this is the case. Of course, the need to maintain appearances is present in all sham, but I believe the other components of it are more variable.

An outstanding example of social sham on a large scale in our society is the condition of the Negro, who lives like a rat, being told he lives in a democracy and that everything is being done to improve his lot; and the ghetto riots are the expression on a social scale of the underlying schizophrenic dialectic. The hostility of the Negro erupts in shooting in the presence of sham, while the clinical schizophrenic, having learnt that he dare not erupt, goes mad, and may shoot himself. On the international scene, of course, the biggest sham is the war in Vietnam, where the United States, while proclaiming to the world that it is building a nation, is destroying one.

Sham arises from fear of retaliation (being 'shot') and because inner restraints interfere with frankness. Sham can derive also from self-deception, in the sense that we believe that by concealing the truth we are doing the other person good. Sham gives rise to coalitions because usually sham cannot be maintained without confederates. The confederate may be a member of the same family, the same organization, or even the same person; for in sham the deceiver enters into an inner conspiracy against a part of himself. Sham makes possible the maintenance of falseness in the face of the dialectic which urges all negations towards resolution. Therefore sham is always static. Outright falsehood can be negated by truth, and one truth leads to another or to a lie, while sham remains protected by ambiguity. It takes root, then, in the relationship between people or within the soul, and spreads.

Children in our culture cannot avoid sham, for adults cannot escape depression, hostility and so on. Since sham consists in one person's withholding information, while implying that the other person should act as if he had it all; since sham consists also in giving false information while expecting the other person to act as if the information were true; since sham consists in deriving advantage from withholding or giving false information – and since, on the whole, our culture is *sham-wise*, it might seem that the main problem for the mental health of children is to familiarize them with the edges of sham. Yet, if we were to do that, they would be 'shot', for Albee is right. Our main problem then is to tell them the world lies but that they should act as if it told the truth. But this too is impossible, for if one acted as if all sham were truth, he might not be shot, but he would certainly lose all his money and marry the wrong person though he would have lots of friends.

What then is the main problem; or rather, what does mankind do? People do not like children who lack innocence, for they hold the mirror up to adults. If children could not be deceived they would threaten adults beyond toleration, they would never be orderly in elementary school and they clearly could not be taught the rot-gut dished out to them as truth.

Personally I do not know what to do; and I anticipate a geometric increase in madness, for sham is at the basis of schizophrenia and murder itself. The sophisticated analysis we have nowadays points ineluctably to one conclusion – that all pathways to schizophrenia cross the mountains, the plains, the deserts, the forests and the fires of sham.

I now distinguish between black sham and white, paralleling the distinction between white magic and black. In anthropology one uses the expression white magic for magic that does good and black magic for magic that harms. In social life white sham helps society get its business done. For example, at a faculty meeting the professors may detest each other, be jealous of one another's success, have secret contempt for one another's work and so on, but they tell jokes, bellow with conventional policy committee laughter, listen seriously to each other's opinions and so on. This is white sham because it gets the departmental business done. They might even smile at each other in the corridor and touch a glass of sherry in the afternoon. Without such sham the necessary administrative tasks could not get done; and nobody is really hurt by it. Black sham arises when Hilfquinkel, Nachtfeuer, Blandishment and Littlefellow get together to plot the overthrow of the chairman, while smiling to his face every day. While adults are all familiar with this distinction between white sham and black, children have to learn it; and in their early days, even in relatively healthy families, they interpret white sham as black: one cannot explain to a child that no harm is intended by the sham, for to him *deception itself is a blow*. Adults, hardened and knowledgeable about sham, cannot understand that what to them is the way of the sham-world is to a child the evil way of the parent. Children have not learnt that he who does not learn to believe sham the truth deserves to be shot. Quite the contrary, they believe that whoever practises sham on *them* deserves to be shot. From adult sham the child derives a feeling of vulnerability – which arises in part from having believed too well.

Meanwhile, by the time he is six years old or so, the child has probably learnt that he will be shot if he does not believe with all his heart and soul that sham IS truth; and the latency period, to the extent that it exists in our culture, is not so much a repression of sexuality as a repression of TRUTH. *Let us be clear about this:* it is not sexuality that is the major repression at six but awareness of the difference between truth and lies. It is not so much that the child has learnt to present a sexless façade to adults as that he has learnt that adults are shams and that he must follow suit, and act as if he did not see – and indeed he must not see. A fundamental error in Freudian psychology is that neurosis derives from the repression of sex when it really derives from the repression of truth.

When a child is very young, in the pre-school years, he learns something about sham from his parents; but his major introduction to sham, at the institutional level, is school, where he learns to give the teacher what she wants. Already in the second grade the teacher knows how to cue the children in so she will not be embarrassed by their disagreeing with her; and part of her art consists in getting the children to understand that in the classroom reality is what the *teacher* wants. This is the fundamental issue at the institutional level; this is the fundamental reality; this is the reality you must have before you the rest of your life if you do not wish to be shot.

To return now to the problem stated at the beginning of this paper, that the main problem of psychiatry is to define sanity and account for its occurrence, I would say that the major problem of psychiatry is to study children who are not too seriously disturbed already in order to learn how they manage to deal with fakery. My feeling is that in this reseach there lies the promise of the discovery of a new universe of human functioning. The first great move forward of the western intellect was made through the Greek examination of the nature of incorrect reasoning. What is enclosed in Socrates' thinking is his unravelling of the nature of the illogical. It is time to return to the Socratic quest. Let us start now with children, who, standing between their own immature faculties and the subterfuges of parents and teachers, are at the centre of world sham. It may be that only a child can see that the emperor has no clothes; but we can be sure that if he said it in public he would be beaten. I do not by any means propose that children be taught to see the truth, for I do not see how adults could teach them. I am merely suggesting that in the interest of mental health it would be important to know how, spontaneously, so many children, knowing the world to be fake, learn how to deal with it without going mad, while others never learn – either that it is a fake or how to deal with it.

In the light of these considerations sanity is nothing more than the capacity to deal with falseness, in a false world; and it can take three forms – Albee's, which is to believe sham to be the truth; to see through sham while using it; or to see through sham but fight it. These three uses constitute three stages in the future social evolution of man: we are now in the stage of believing sham to be the truth, while entering the stage of seeing through sham while using it. The third stage is understanding sham and knowing how to fight it. The fourth stage is a world without sham.

8. Forty-Year-Old Jitters in Married Urban Women*

I. Introduction

It seems to me that I learnt about a disease called involutional melancholia when I began to attend grand rounds at a psychiatric hospital in the mid-1930s. In those days I learnt that involutional melancholia was a psychotic depression afflicting ageing women; that it came upon them like cancer; that it was organically determined and that it was just as difficult to cure as cancer. Involutional melancholia, I was told, was a function of organic decay, somehow related to the female reproductive system, and nothing could be done about the onset, though there might be some hope of recovery – just as there was for cancer. As we have learnt more about emotional illness, however, we have dropped the notion of inevitability, and incurability; and our assurance about physical determinants has decreased in proportion as our sensitivity to environmental factors and our capacity to discriminate among patterns of illness has increased. The so-called involutional melancholia, the deep depression that sometimes afflicts ageing women, can no longer be viewed as a simple consequence of a physiological ageing that has merely reached an extreme in some cases but

* Prepared for the conference on the consequences for women of urbanization, University of California School of Medicine, January 1965. Reprinted from Seymour M. Farber and Roger H. L. Wilson (eds.), *The Challenge to Women* (New York, 1966).

must be seen as a disease in which the environment is important, and which is an extreme expression of a lesser, but widespread, disturbance in most women as a consequence of ageing in our culture.

Emotional illness we know is a phenomenon of vulnerability; and we express this conviction by saying that people become emotionally ill when their defences either break down or are too rigid. Society defends most of us against attacks from within and without by giving us a role and a reasonably good opinion of ourselves, by surrounding us with friends and so on. Since in the woman of forty or so many of these culturally determined defences are crumbling, so that the feeling of vulnerability grows and sometimes becomes acute to the point of serious impairment of function – involutional, in other words – it is important to review what a woman's culturally determined defences are, and how, one by one, they may be swept away, leaving her standing alone and unprotected.

Just as a physician looks at the functioning of the body when he deals with illness so the social scientist must look to society. Obviously, for example, the causes of venereal disease, tuberculosis, cholera, typhoid and even of measles and most other diseases are social as well as physiological; and the social scientist, asked to discuss the misery of ageing women, must just as surely look for the causes of it in the culture as the physician must look for them in the body. In this case, as in most cases of emotional upset, the social scientist is probably closer to the truth than the usual physician. I shall therefore outline what I consider to be the cultural sources of the female misery called forty-year-old jitters. I begin with some general features of our social organization.

II. *Our Socio-Economic Structure Isolates People*

While some people may be driven mad by those around them, most of mankind is not, but rather finds a personal community a necessary condition of existence. Yet societies around the world vary enormously in the degree to which they guarantee everyone a personal community – a group of people on whom one can rely for approval and support.[1] For example, the families of traditional China and contemporary peasant India are extended so that one can count on a group of people related to one through one's father. Beyond that, in traditional China, was the wider reach of the lineage or clan – the even more extended group of paternal relatives. Peasant India extends the network even further, to the caste – the people united through similar occupation and religious observances. One of the most astonishing facts of social life is that almost the entire populations of China and India lived for uncountable ages under this family type we call in anthropology the joint family. Evidently it has given such shelter, security and comfort that, with all its internal stresses, it has survived for centuries. It is only one example of the variety of forms of permanent and sheltering kinship structures that have protected mankind against starvation, loneliness and discard.

When we turn to the societies of the contemporary West, and to much of the Soviet Union and its allies, we discover radically different conditions, for in industrialized nations one is not born, as the Chinese were, and as most peasant Indians are today, to a supporting personal community that can not turn its face away.[2] Among us extended obligatory mutual involvements are rare and we are not even obliged by law to support our parents – a monstrous condition when viewed from the perspective of India or traditional China, or indeed in the historic perspective of mankind. Thus in our culture there is no guarantee that we will never stand alone. Only the ringing of

1. See Jules Henry, 'The Personal Community and Its Invariant Properties', *American Anthropologist*, Vol. LX, 1960, pp. 827–31.

2. I am aware that there are still some relatively stable enclaves even in industrial centres nowadays. Even these, however, lack the stability of tribal and most peasant societies.

the telephone tells the urban dweller a friend is calling, reminding the family that they are not alone.

Nevertheless there is always the danger that the phone will cease to ring. People die – particularly as we grow older – or move away, and there is scarcely a writer on American life who has not commented on our enormous historic mobility in space; and now we know that it is not only spatial mobility that disunites people, but movement up or down in the social scale, so that some people who mixed with us yesterday no longer call us because they have become too important. The same is true of our own behaviour: too often we value people not so much because they are loyal but because they are somebody.

Finally we are separated from one another by *middle-class intangibles* – the trivia of personality that make us say, with a shrug or a grimace, 'I don't know – there is something about Mary . . . I can't put my finger on it, but I can't stand her any more. We used to be good friends, but she has a way . . . I don't know whether it's what she says or the way she says it . . . And then her husband. . . I remember when they were first married, he seemed such a nice man but now . . . Maybe it's because of her . . .' And so it goes; the reason for the break is never quite known either to the person who breaks off or to the one who is dropped. We are a people committed to evanesce; it makes it easier to separate. But this impermanence of relationships also isolates us from one another. On the other hand, however, what ills life brings are easier to bear when we are not alone; and thus it comes about that so many women have so few people they can rely on, that when the phantasms of ageing begin to gather, they must fight them alone – without an extended and protecting personal community.

III. *Ours is a Child- Rather than a Parent-Centred Society*

Having spoken of the family structures of China and India I have only begun to discuss the advantages for adults in such families. China and India are parent-centred societies, while ours is child-centred. This difference is expressed beautifully in *Twenty-Four Examples of Filial Piety*,[3] a book of lessons about family life studied by children in traditional China.

For example:

Tale IV

Resigns Post (to)[4] Seek Mother

When Chu Shou-chang . . . was seven years of age, his mother left the family and remarried because of the jealousy of her husband's other wife. Thereafter mother and son did not see each other for fifty years. At last . . . Chu Shou-chang gave up his official post . . . having sworn to his own family that he would not return unless he found his mother. (His) travels took him to the prefecture of Tungchou, and there he met his mother, who was then more than seventy years old.

Tale VII

Weeps (among) Bamboos (and) Sprouts Grow

In the kingdom of Wu lived Meng Tsung. His father had died when he was young, and his mother was aged and very sick. During the winter months she longed for soup made of bamboo sprouts, but Tsung found no way to obtain them. Then he went to a grove, where he embraced the bamboos and wept. His filial piety moved Heaven and Earth, and all of a sudden the ground burst open and a few sprouts sprang up. Bringing them home, he cooked a soup for his mother; and when she had eaten it she found herself *well*.

Tale XV

For Mother's Sake, (He) Buried (his) Son

Ko Chü . . . who was very poor, had a son three years of age. Ko

3. See 'A Primer of Filial Piety', Mischa Titiev and Hsing-Chih Tien (eds) in *Papers of the Michigan Academy of Science, Arts and Letters*, Vol. XXXIII, 1947.

4. Elements in parentheses are not present in a literal translation from the Chinese and have been added by the editors to make good English.

Chü's mother (used to) cut down on her own food in order to provide more for her grandson. (At last Ko Chü) said to his wife: 'We are so poor that we cannot (properly) support our mother. Furthermore, our son shares mother's food. Why not bury this son. We can have sons again, but never (another) mother.' His wife did not dare to disobey.

One day Chü dug a hole more than three feet deep. Suddenly he saw a piece of yellow gold on which were inscribed characters reading: 'Heaven sent this yellow gold to the filial son, Ko Chü. Let no official confiscate it, and let no citizen take it away from him.'

It is clear that in the culture portrayed in these stories a mother did not suffer, as many do among us, from the loss of her mature children. Though these are but tales, and represent unattainable ideals, they do express much of the essence of family life in old China – a parent-centred society.

Along with parent-centredness went ancestor-centredness, a devout and conforming attitude towards ancestors that so anchored the culture in the past that new generations differed little from old ones, and children, parents, grandparents and departed ancestors had so much in common that the domestic cleavage and communications block we find between generations in our culture – a blockage that isolates parents from children and causes conflict – could not arise to separate the generations and make a mother feel lonely and cast aside. It is true that the parent-ancestor-centred society changed with great difficulty and that the personalities of family members were submerged by adherence to the family ideal, yet we pay a toll in loneliness and conflict for our own individualistic type of family.

IV. *The Metaphysic of Youth, Beauty and Romantic Love*

The emphasis on youth, beauty and romantic love is a sustaining force in our economy. While it is ancient, having roots in the

Judeo-Christian and Greek traditions[5] – this emphasis, amounting to an implied metaphysic, has reached unparalleled expansive significance in our economy, which must monetize everything in order to remain viable. Without the pecuniary exploitation of romantic love and female youth and beauty the women's wear, cosmetics and beauty-parlour industries would largely disappear and the movies, TV and phonograph-record businesses would on the whole cease to be economically functional, degenerating, perhaps, to the relative economic insignificance of education. It is true that women would still need clothes to protect themselves from the elements, and that civilization demands that they cover their bodies even in hot weather; but the billions spent on women's wear these days is more in the interest of making women attractive than in protecting them from the cold. Furthermore, without the erotizing effects of the metaphysic of youth, beauty and romantic love, cigarettes, hard and soft drinks, beer, automobiles and so on would not sell nearly as well. As a matter of fact, even men's wear and toiletries could not be marketed as efficiently without an adoring, pretty woman (well under thirty-five years of age) looking at a man wearing a stylish shirt or sniffing at a man wearing a deodorant.

While the saturation of the pecuniary media with the metaphysic of youth, beauty and romantic love should not be attacked, lest the economy collapse – just as if we suddenly attacked the profit motive; and while the metaphysic speeds up courtship and the birthrate, thus adding further to expenditures and to the gross national product, obsession with youth, beauty and romantic love punishes the woman who, having reached

5. While Abraham became a hero as an older man, subsequent heroes and heroines were mostly young: Jacob, Deborah, Benjamin, David, Moses, etc. Christ was yet a child when he confounded the priests; his disciples were young, and Christ was yet young when he died on the cross. Only the miserable role of prophet seems to have been reserved for older men. The role of young and beautiful men in Plato is familiar.

thirty-five, begins to see in the mirror the fact that the metaphysic and its implied defences no longer exist for her. We have a metaphysic for beauty and youth but none for the years when these are gone. In this sense the West is probably unique; for while throughout history culture has provided a set of principles for guidance through every stage of life, in the contemporary West ageing hangs in nothingness. For many a woman of thirty-five and beyond therefore it is as if the universe had physically withdrawn and left her hurtling into nothingness. And thus, deprived of the youth, beauty and romantic love, which once made them feel safe, many women feel they have no place to go but down.

Since a metaphysic is a system of first principles underlying a subject of inquiry, since our subject of inquiry is urban woman, and since she is without a metaphysic after forty, we are bound to state what the metaphysic was in the first place. It should be mentioned, in passing, that it is not necessary that a metaphysic be 'true', for it can just as well be a system of principles supporting a false position; and the history of thought has shown that this is usually the case.

The metaphysic of which I speak embodies the following principles: 1. A man validates himself by working and supporting; a woman validates herself by getting a man. 2. A man does, a woman is. Man performs; woman attracts. Behind this principle lies the fact that urban woman has lost most of her productive economic functions; and even when she does productive labour, the money she earns is used largely to expand the family's life style rather than to create fundamental conditions for living. 3. Existence must be made aesthetically pleasing. 4. Since man's province is that of action, it is up to the woman to make life aesthetically attractive to him, and to display his masculinity by being attractive. 5. From all this it follows that women must be beautiful. 6. Since beauty is by definition physical and since the body loses its freshness even before the end of the child-bearing years, a woman is in danger of losing her husband in this period. To these principles, deriving from the metaphysic of youth and beauty, add the following from romantic love. 7. Since in our culture marriage is not arranged by parents and the spouse is not determined by highly specific social rules, every woman must find and attract a husband for herself. Often in traditional peasant China a girl did not see her husband before the wedding day, for the marriage was arranged by the parents. In many tribal cultures, on the other hand, a girl's husband is selected for her, even before birth, because she has to marry a specific person according to rules prescribed by tradition. 8. Romantic love is based on obsession with the beloved, to the exclusion of all others, and requires the idealization of the object. It is clear meanwhile that grand obsession and idealization can rarely withstand the rigours of marriage. It follows from principles 7 and 8 that as youth and beauty wane and as the realities of marriage erode obsession and idealization, urban woman in our culture is bound to become uneasy, for what once seemed to protect her from nothingness seems to be going away.

Summing up, in a somewhat oversimplified way: as long as a woman has little to offer but her physical person, love as obsession and idealization will fade as she gets old and as the daily collisions of marriage make living together difficult or merely routine.

Since in our urban culture marriage is not consolidated through cooperative work but through a complicated hallucination of intangibles based on obsession and idealization, the loss of youth and beauty may appear to threaten a woman whose youth and beauty are passing. Meanwhile, since she probably knows many cases in which an older man has deserted his wife for a younger and more attractive woman, a wife cannot but ask, 'When will it happen to me?'

V. *The Devaluation of Children*

I have pointed out that historically society has swung between two extreme types of parent-child relations – parent-centred and child-centred. It may seem a paradox that in parent-centred societies children are more valued than in child-centred ones, but a moment's reflection shows that far from being a paradox such a high valuation on children is a necessary consequence of a parent-centred society. In parent-centred societies the child is bound to support his parents – never to desert them; and this binding is partly in very rigid economic terms, for children, especially sons, must provide for parents. Hence it would be folly, besides being shameful, for a father to desert his children. The economic obligation however, is reinforced by the requirement that the sons perform the ceremonies necessary for the tranquil and comfortable existence of the father's soul in the next world – double reason for never deserting the children. In a child-centred culture the only thing binding parents and children is the vulnerable love relationship. Hence if a father who wants a new love affair decides he does not need his children's love there is nothing other than legalities to keep him home. Thus when the youth and beauty of his wife have faded, the attractions of a new and younger love may overwhelm a man's attachment to his children because they are not a necessary condition of his existence here and in the hereafter.

This brings us to the problems of the husband.

VI. *The Husband's Situation*

So far I have considered only the woman's vulnerability; but her vulnerability has to be considered in relation to her husband's. There are many factors in a man's life at the age of forty that make him anxious and may cause him to turn to a young and pretty woman for comfort and reassurance; so that just as the vulnerability system is making his wife fearful, it is pressing her husband so hard that the very circumstance she fears may indeed hasten upon her. We know, for example, that in the man's occupational world emphasis is on the young and 'coming', so that a man of forty may be looking anxiously over his shoulder at the wolf pack yapping and slobbering at his heels as he slips along over competitive business ice. At forty the status of many a man, whether in business or on the assembly line, is frozen, so he feels stuck and fearful. So also, especially if he is in one of the 'creative' professions, he may feel that his powers are lessening. Hence, driven by anxieties, he may turn to a young and pretty woman for reassurance; and as she comes to him she gives him a feeling that after all he is not lost: he is not as weak as he thinks. She will, he feels, give him new creative powers, because her sex interest proves he is not dead wood. It is a commonplace that sex narcotizes anxiety; and when numerous illusions dress it up it can seem *the* solution to all a man's problems.

There is also the special illusion that appears under the slogan, 'Life is to be lived'; and for the man who does not find satisfaction in his work; who has done what he has had to do rather than what he wanted to do; or whose life work has turned out not to be what he thought it was; or whose inherent feelings of nothingness are too great for any work to defeat – for any such man the cure to his life-long disorder may seem to be the young and beautiful woman. The tragedy is that just when his wife needs him most, a man's own tragedy may leave him with less and less to give her.

Yet even the successful man may intensify his wife's anxiety, for as he drives himself in his business and career, as these continue to make enormous demands on his time and energy, his absorption may seem to confirm his wife's worst anxieties. Interpreting his preoccupation as a turning away from her, she may become a nag or importune him when he is involved in other things, and this starts a vicious cycle; for the more she protests that he does not love her, the more she importunes when his mind is on his affairs, the more irritated he may become, with consequent mutual withdrawal and an increase in the wife's anxiety.

VII. The Loss of Maternal Functions[6]

As the children grow up they not only don't need their mother as much as they used to – they may positively resent her intervention in their lives – except, of course, when she intervenes on their side to get the father to consent to something. Recently I saw the following on TV at 9 a.m.: Mrs Jones has bought Dotty a low-cut formal gown as a present for her thirteenth birthday; and Dotty has got a date with a boy who is going to take her dancing to a swank hotel. High heels and lipstick enhance the formal. Now Daddy, who has been away on a trip, comes home, and is outraged by the whole idea – low-cut dress, lipstick, heels – and the swank hotel. He is defeated in the ensuing argument because his wife sides with Dotty. Just before I tuned out, Daddy had fallen asleep in the living-room and had a dream in which Dotty is a call-girl, and he is beaten up by her pimp.

This skit expresses a great deal about American family life; but what is particularly important for our present interest is Mrs Jones's 'late maternal function'; for now she attempts to bind her daughter to her by taking sides with her against the father. Obviously Mrs Jones, who is clearly at the dangerous age, can only intensify her problems with her husband as she tries to find a new way of establishing herself with a daughter who no longer needs her the way she did five years ago.

Our contemporary small families no longer require long-range exercise of simple maternal functions; for the few children

6. Some of the problems raised here and in Section 9 have been anticipated and discussed by Betty Friedan in *The Feminine Mystique*, especially in Chapter 14.

soon learn to take care of themselves. This leaves the mother with nothing to do in the family but meddle in her children's lives. This in turn is related to two things. In the first place it is no longer chic to continue having children after you have passed thirty-five. Such fertility may make the neighbours wonder whether Mrs So-and-so 'doesn't know when to stop'. The notion of 'meddling' in children's lives is in turn related to permissive attitudes towards children, to the freeing of the sexual impulses, to the increase in allowances for fun expenditures, to the idea that parents and children are equals – so that mother and father are now more like older sister and brother – and to the children's discovery that they can undermine parental authority by ganging up under the slogan, 'Mary Smith's mother lets her do it, why don't you let me do it?' In this way children have snatched power from parental hands; and instead of children fearing loss of parental love, urban American parents fear loss of their children's. Children can gang up on parents simply because they are united in the peer group while parents are disunited – among neighbours and within families.

What drives the message home is that the mobilization of the adolescent cohorts occurs just when the mother is worried that because she is past her peak her husband won't love her. What makes her anxiety worse is her knowledge that giving in because she is afraid her adolescent children will be angry may alienate her husband: if she lets the children have their way over her husband's objections he may not forgive her – especially if the consequences are serious. The fundamental issue is that just as the urban woman becomes more dependent on her husband, she is beginning to collide with her adolescent children.

At the present time we are perhaps witnessing an intensification of these problems because early marriage and the early cessation of child-bearing leave a woman without maternal functions even sooner than before.

VIII. *Menopause as Symbolic Decline*

I am under the impression that even nowadays menopause may symbolize to many women that they have somehow ceased to be women. Formerly involutional melancholia was viewed by the medical profession as an expectable consequence of the physiology of menopause. Surely, to the degree that such depression is related to menopause, it must be largely in a symbolic sense, rather than a hormonal one. Surely menopause must mean to such women that since they are no longer good for children they are good for nothing; and surely to them menopause must be more of a symbolic than a physiologic decline. A central issue is the over-evaluation of fertility, because so many women have not been trained for anything else; because they have been given no other goal than home and children. Of equal importance is their feeling that having reached menopause they will go rapidly downhill, losing all attractiveness.

IX. *The Frustration of Earlier Ambitions and the Lack of Preparation for Later Life*

The process through which a woman gives up early ambitions for marriage has been mentioned by Betty Friedan in *The Feminine Mystique*. Duty to her womanhood, a real desire for a home and children, fear that she will never be able to realize career dreams, and even a desire to be taken care of because fundamentally she fears life, all make their contribution to that complex sensation of love, guilt, yearning and anxiety with which many women enter marriage. At any rate, however complex her feelings may be, many a woman gets married with the idea that some day, after her children no longer need her, she will return to her original hopes for herself. As the years pass, however, as one child follows upon another, with all the hardship that raising a family and coping with her husband involve, it becomes ever clearer to her that the early ambition will never be realized. This loss of hope contributes to her misery.

Everything is made worse by the fact that women are given no training in keeping the Self alive. Quite the contrary, woman in our culture is trained in renunciation; it is her destiny to give up: to give up for her husband and to give up for her children. All the lovingly acquired knowledge of the French Renaissance poets disappears easily in fifteen years; and the hands that held a violin bow or paint brush may have lost their elasticity in the endless round of household chores. The deadliest influence of all is to have married a troglodyte, for, however loving he may be, a dull husband is poison to the intellect. Thus the woman discovers that she has made no preparation for later life: she has not kept her gifts alive – and nobody has insisted that she ought to. All of this is happening while her children grow up and need her no more and her husband is having his own forty-year-old jitters.

X. *Egoistic versus Public-Oriented Work*

Betty Friedan's examination of the life and hopes of college-educated women over forty or so is heavily weighted in favour of the women with special talents and job desires, and thus overlooks the mass of women who lack both, but who find during the later years that simply taking care of the house and engaging in voluntary work – the most easily available work after thirty-five – is not satisfying.

While much of the work a homemaker can do outside the home is voluntary and unpaid, this is precisely the type of work women interviewed by Friedan end up despising. There are two kinds of work: egoistic work, which one enjoys because it gives deep satisfaction or because one gets paid; and work oriented towards others and motivated by the desire to help them. Activities available to untrained women, even though they be college graduates, are mostly of the latter kind. Friedan's women – and perhaps most women – belittle work on local committees, on parent-teacher associations, and so on, while yearning for careers in egoistic activities. The problem here is that, except for top-level jobs, our culture has never valued public-oriented work. Just as we readily spend on egoistic consumption – on things that contribute directly to pleasure and comfort – and are stingy about spending for public benefits, so we are contemptuous of work not immediately gratifying to the self-image, even though the gratification is merely in being paid. So it is that a trivial job for which a woman is paid, even though she doesn't need the money, seems more rewarding than a public-oriented job for which she receives no pay. Since industry needs paid labour and people who will spend their pay on what industry produces, we have been taught that what is significant is egoistic work, and that public service is, on the whole, contemptible and is mostly for people who couldn't make it any other way; and all our lives we have been told that what counts is money income. It is absurd to expect women to derive a sense of fulfilment from a job that is public-oriented and unpaid.

A possible solution to the problem is to emphasize public service in the college courses and to make some public service obligatory for all students. Even better would be to pay people for doing the jobs that are now voluntary. This, however, requires greater public willingness to spend on public services. In a large hospital in my town the coffee shop is run largely by upper-middle-class women volunteers. It is true that this saves the hospital money, but it is also true that if people weren't so stingy with money that might go to the hospital, the women would be paid. But this, in turn, would deprive those who really need the jobs. The solution is obviously expanded federal subsidies to hospitals.

XI. *Summary and Conclusions*

The predicament of the woman of forty or so is the product of a culture that provides her with few defences as she grows older. Or, put another way, the illusions and the realities that stabilized her through earlier years are swept away. Such a state of affairs owes its existence to the economy and to the flight of philosophy from life. Throughout history philosophy has not examined the nature of folk metaphysics because philosophy has rejected 'the many'. The analytical capabilities of philosophy must be brought to bear on folk metaphysics.

'Forty-year-old jitters' are the result of the imposition of the primordial image of the big-bellied, heavy-breasted, fat-hipped figure of the paleolithic caves on contemporary life. This image, basically unchanged, except for slimming and uplifting features introduced by modern cosmetic technology, still dominates thinking about women. Nowadays, however, there is too much more for her to do than what is represented by the caves and even her vast reproductive capabilities are obsolescent. In the old Stone Age when the race needed women who could reproduce frequently in order to overcome the high infant death rate – when it was multiply or perish; when survival of species and tribe was determined by the fact that when two biological forms live in the same habitat and use the environment in the same way, the form that reproduces faster will win; when a man lost the next world as well as this one if he had no children – when man existed under these conditions, high fertility was important and so were other primordial maternal functions. This past has been preserved in altered form in the folk ideology that binds the modern housewife, making her vulnerable to forty-year-old jitters – the disease of modernity and urbanism.

When children meant hands to work the field, sons to track

and kill animals, destroy the enemy and carry on the ancestor cult; when daughters were for house and field and to sell off to buy wives for sons; and when all was threatened by a high infant mortality, reproductive capability was vital. And when occupations were few, it made sense to keep woman bound to her functions in house and field. But nowadays occupational possibilities for women have increased more than a thousand-fold[7] and the necessary qualifications are diverse enough to suit every woman.

It is useless to attack this position on the grounds that since our society is running out of jobs for men because of automation, anything that gets women out of traditional roles will contribute to a masculine employment crisis. In the first place, in America we misuse automation, for instead of using the increased productivity resulting from it to lower prices and expand consumption, and hence production and employment, it is being employed to displace workers, while much of the savings made possible by the new techniques are distributed in profits. This has always been the case when new technology has been invented, and it usually takes a century and terrifying depressions to alter the situation. In the second place, government does not adequately subsidize labour. Since government subsidizes the armaments industry, backbone of the economy, air transportation, agriculture and shipping, among other industries; since it has given great subsidies to the railroads, through land grants; since it subsidizes oil through generous depletion allowances and so on, government subsidy for labour is long overdue. For over a century government subsidy to industry has been a commonplace, but labour has been subsidized only in times of dire need; when indeed it was absolutely necessary in order to renew purchasing power, as an indirect

7. The latest census gives 296 basic occupations, each divided into so many subsidiary ones that there are thousands. See 1960 *Census of Population. Alphabetical Index of Occupations and Industries (Revised)*. US Department of Commerce, Bureau of the Census.

subsidy to industry. Subsidies to labour must become as matter of course as subsidies to industry.

Thus we must not be bamboozled by 'the spectre of automation', for it becomes manageable when viewed against the background of all economic possibilities, including the gigantic powers of government.

The simple fact is that an exclusively private-enterprise economy is no longer able to use all our human potentialities. The paradox inheres in the fact that private enterprise, while liberating many creative powers in man and woman, often leaves them unused because unilateral adherence to the profit motive creates unemployment and dead-end jobs. Meanwhile, again paradoxically, as Betty Friedan points out, the unused potential of women is ploughed back into industrial profits through advertising's plugging 'creative housekeeping'.

Nowadays the woman of forty is a casualty of the metaphysics of youth, beauty and romantic love, and of a conception of woman's functions having roots in the Stone Age. Until the beginning of the twentieth century we were filling up a vast country, and children and mothers died early because of poor sanitation, ignorance and hard work. Meanwhile, however, industry has pumped humanity out of all of Europe to man our new industrial machine – even sending recruiters abroad and combining with steamship companies to stimulate the poor of Europe to come to America, land of promise. We do not need fast increase of population any more. Furthermore the concept of work has shifted from survival through work to satisfaction in work. Along with this change must go the question about woman's role in the home: is it necessary for the survival of the family or is it necessary for her satisfaction as a woman? Such considerations, examined by Betty Friedan, are inseparable from the problem of forty-year-old jitters.

Why does psychoanalysis cling to the idea that housewifely dissatisfaction is an expression of 'rejection of the feminine role'? In the first place, most psychoanalysts are like everybody else – they are nice people trying to get along. Why should they question outworn ideas they learnt in school? In the second place, the woman who is miserable because her family role no longer gives her satisfaction looks to them like a kind of delinquent; for she has stepped out of line, just like a kid who smokes marijuana. Furthermore every dissatisfied and jittery wife could be the analyst's wife: How would *he* feel if when *he* came home everything was not in ship-shape – as must be the case often when a wife has outside interests? Fighting the housewife patient who wants to get out of the house therefore has a certain virtuous puritanism about it; but the psycho-analytic belief in the metaphysical necessity of the stereotypic feminine role inevitably collides with the destructive con-sequences for the woman of forty of the metaphysic of youth, beauty and romantic love, and with the real opportunities of urban life, particularly for college women.

Yet, on the other hand, what would happen to our economy if the metaphysic of youth, beauty and romantic love were to vanish? Building airships to carry two thousand people; or even criss-crossing all of Central America with canals would not save us. Thus has psychoanalytic conservatism become a bulwark of the economy. In their own way they are as necessary to it as the engineers.

To avoid forty-year-old jitters middle-class women must be trained for later life – for the time when their children no longer need them; and they must not be permitted to forget that as children grow to puberty in contemporary America, the maternal function has little reward; and that guidance is resented by the children they have liberated by their permissive-ness. At all stages suitable educational materials must be pro-vided women so their minds will not go to pot. It is striking that while even the cereal-and-toy-vending television pro-grammes for little children are interlarded here and there with educational bits, daytime programmes for housewives are strictly at the visceral level. Educational daytime shows for those soon to become victims of the youth-beauty-romantic-love metaphysic, however, would sell more hair spray, bath oil, cake mixes, bacon, shortening, refrigerators and so on than a dozen *Peyton Places*, because they would not be nearly so depressing. Women ought to be acquainted with their predicament and coached on how to get out of it. Back to school programmes for women are very good, but as a college teacher I know that some who come back at forty don't have much of a brain any more, although many, of course, do. On the other hand, how many thousands who might like to come back do we never see at all because their minds have lost elasticity during twenty years of marriage?

The forty-year-old wife of the blue-collar worker is probably no different.[8]

In closing, I return to involutional melancholia. It is not biology but the life-long cumulative effects of a punitive and uncomprehending environment impinging on the vulnerabilities of ageing that cause this disease. Yet the victims themselves are part of its causation, because so many of them believe that all they should have to offer is youth, beauty, romantic love and children, and because many of them have entered marriage as an escape from taking responsibility for themselves.

8. See 'Mental Health in the Workers' World', by Claude C. Bowman in *Blue Collar World*, Arthur B. Shostak and William Gomberg (eds), (New York, 1964), p. 374.

9. The United States: From Barbarism to Decadence without Civilization?*

The title of this lecture series is 'Man's Potential: Vision Unlimited', but we must always have the gravest doubts about any notion of limitlessness when applied to what is concrete – like man, for example. In the United States the devastation of our land by deforestation, by over-cultivation and by over-grazing, the destruction of our fish and game, the pollution of our water and air testify to the catastrophe implicit in the notion of the limitlessness of the concrete, and suggest that, mistaking his insatiable appetite for limitless vision, man has projected this hallucination upon nature, so that, relative to his insatiability, nature herself has seemed merely an inexhaustible reserve waiting to be plundered. When the immigrants from the Old World came to the New World they seemed to perceive nature unlimited. The streams swarmed with fish, the forests appeared boundless, and they teemed with wild animals and birds. The western plains of North America, from Texas to Canada, shook beneath the hooves of millions of bison. The air was so pure after the disease and stench of the great cities of Europe and the water so sweet that it seemed as if a paradise of inexhaustibleness had indeed presented itself on earth to those who, deprived in body and soul, poured into America. The degradation to which many colonists had been subjected in the Old World

* Based on an address prepared for the Canadian Centennial, University of British Columbia, Vancouver, 11 March 1967.

combined with the immemorial insatiability of Man-in-the-West to create an 'unlimited vision' of nature passively awaiting appropriation. Man-in-the-West then immediately set about *limiting* the indigenous population by killing it off. About *this* particular product of nature he had no hallucination for it stood in the way of his insatiability and the remnant of that resource lives out its miserable limitations among us today. The so-called vision of the white man, which is often nothing more than his insatiability projected, as the delusion of limitlessness, on to nature, has almost entirely eliminated the red man. The deculturated American Indian is in human form exactly the same as our degraded and exhausted natural resources. The concrete elimination of the Indians and forests, the erosion of land, the destruction of wild life and the pollution of waters and air are witness, on the one hand, to the reality of limitation and on the other, to the inherent antagonism between insatiability and nature, between the hallucinations of man and the reality on which he acts them out. Having experienced the limitations in the concrete *actuality* we must not continue to fall back on the unlimited nature of *vision*. The spirit is nothing more than what culture, that is, man himself, makes it, and if culture stamps out courage, solicitude and universality, a vision of man that ignores national boundaries, his spirit is nothing; but not nothing in the sense of a beginning, but nothing in the sense of being dead. I shall return to this conception of the essence of spirit.

The idea of limitlessness, boundlessness and timelessness has a long history in our culture, but what is most important for the present discussion is the fate of man when he attaches that idea to himself or to anything he touches. Almost as long as we have written records we get a sense of man's intuition of limit-lessness, so that it is no wonder that he not only has come to perceive the universe as limitless but has thought of himself that way too. This is the tragic error, and, my colleague Professor Albert Hofstater tells me, this view of man is considered akin to paganism in some contemporary religious philosophy.

Meanwhile man has turned his intuition of his own unlimited nature into religion, science, business, imperialism, profits, war, dispoliation and death. That is to say that the concept of limit-lessness has often become transformed into insatiability by the alchemy of the mind. Thus science itself and notions of un-limited vision have become insidious inner transformations of the idea of infinity. I doubt that the idea of the unlimited working out of any human endeavour is of any value any longer. Since man has, on the basis of the assumption of unlimited potential, finally succeeded in creating the possibility of his own *instantaneous* annihilation, it would seem that the idea of infinity, as applied to human endeavour, has run its course. Over a century ago Alfred Lord Tennyson expressed the same misgivings in his poem *Locksley Hall*:

For I dipt into the future, far as human eye could see,
Saw the Vision of the world, and all the wonder that would be;
Saw the heavens filled with commerce, argosies of magic sails,
Pilots of the purple twilight, dropping down with costly bales;
Heard the heavens filled with shouting, and there rained a ghastly
   dew
From the nations' airy navies, grappling in the central blue.

It is a paradox of history, philosophy and of existence itself, that the infinite leads to the infinitesimal, for the notion of infinite power, as expressed through nuclear fission, has eventuated in the possibility of the total annihilation of man in infinitesimal time. Prophetically, or symbolically, infinitesimal time is expressed in an instantaneous burst of destructive fire. This comes about through the fact that man has always used his discoveries against himself, but I shall speculate that the causes go deeper still. There is no doubt that the capacities of the intellect are immense, and the splitting of the atom, the plumbing of space and the discovery of the underlying chemis-try of life, suggest that intellect has something in it akin to limitlessness. Such material discoveries are paralleled by dis-coveries in the realm of spirit: I put in this category first and foremost the prophets of the Old and the New Testament. The explorations in ideas by Socrates, Plato, Hegel, Kierkegaard and Freud also imply the possibility of a kind of ultimate insight into the nature of reason and of spiritual things in general. Yet these men are a pitiful minority; a minority that has escaped the intellectual sabotage carried out on us by culture. Meanwhile powerful intellectual capabilities are part of the genetic capacities of most of us. Thus insatiability is really the channelling of profound spiritual disappointment and frustration into what culture presents to us as a sop, in the visible, concrete and apparent. Boundless disappointment begets unlimited greed. What urges man on therefore is disappointment; and fear – a fear that he might, deprived of a chance to realize his spiritual potentialities, become non-human. The wellspring of insatiability is therefore disappointment in one's own potentialities. From this flows, in the first place, destruction of others, and, in the final working out of it, destruction of self: the transformation of the human into the inhuman through fear of being non-human.

The modern idea of space is an idea of boundlessness, and the phrase 'the conquest of space' expresses man's feeling that he can make limitless space his own because he himself has limitless capabilities. Surely the phrase 'man in space' means that man has possessed space because he is equal to it. We already know the destructive possibilities inherent in this new possession and the treaty between the United States and the Soviet Union in which they agree – temporarily, at least – to disarm space, expresses our fear of the devastating potential of the latest manifestation of limitlessness. We know already something about what havoc man can wreak even on space itself. Nuclear fall-out is one example and the disturbance of the Van Allen radiation bands is another. Man has done so much damage to earth there is no reason why he might not injure space as seriously. As a matter of fact, earth is itself a part of space.

Meanwhile we perceive, even now, in the United States,

important indirect, destructive consequences of preoccupation with space. Dr Warren Weaver, one of the discoverers of information theory, the mathematical underpinning of automation, said the following about our space race in an article in the *New York Times* of 1 January 1965. With the $30 billion we are to spend in getting to the moon by 1970, he said,

We could give every teacher in the US a 10 per cent raise a year for 10 years; endow 200 small colleges with $10 million each; finance the education through graduate school of 50,000 scientists at $4,000 a year; build 10 new medical schools at $200 million each; build and endow complete universities for more than 50 developing countries; create three new Rockefeller Foundations worth $500 million each.

Thus in the process of achieving or reaching out towards infinity, we undercut ourselves and the rest of the world, for we desperately need what we are compelled to forgo in order to 'conquer' space. Put another way, in conquering space – that is, in stealing space, for conquest is nothing but a theft – we actually rob ourselves in important other respects.

I think we will all admit that enlightenment is one of the most important characteristics of civilization and that the acquisition of knowledge is the pathway to enlightenment; yet the paradox of man is that on the one hand, in the very process of acquiring knowledge, he may be preparing the instrument of his own annihilation, while, on the other, he limits the possibility of knowledge by withdrawing funds from education. It is clear that, at least in my country, man's vision is not unlimited but alarmingly limited. It has a kind of momentary, emotional, rather immature quality, this vision of man, for he sees only what his culture presents to him as most desirable at the moment, and he pursues it blindly.

Another paradox created by limitless aspirations is that the mind of man is often put to work to undo the damage done by his limited vision. Substitutes have to be found for the wood that is no longer available because of deforestation, land must be rehabilitated, floods caused by vicious land use must be controlled, air and water must be purified and techniques invented, legislation passed and money appropriated in order to avoid further pollution, blighted urban areas must be renewed and so on. Money and brains that might be directed towards the civilizing process and towards the relief of miseries inherent in the very process of living are thus used up in order to rescue man from the consequences of his own *limited vision*.

The economic system is the principal pathway along which man-in-the-West has attempted to satisfy his insatiability. That is to say, he has created capitalism, an institution in which insatiable appetite, fused with notions of unlimited potentialities, brought forth the idea of limitless profit. Capitalist economic institutions are instruments for putting into action the idea of profits unlimited, on the other hand, not until capitalist institutions were *formed* was the *idea* of infinite profit possible. Economic institutions, like any others, once established, however, take on the quality of eternal order and the will of God Himself, so that questioning their validity and inherent rightness appears a threat to the foundations of civilization. Hence the emergence of anti-intellectualism, the enemy of questioning and of enlightenment. Aristophanes' *The Clouds* is one of the earliest examples of the relationship between profits and anti-intellectualism, for in that play Aristophanes portrays Socrates as instructing his pupils in how to talk themselves out of paying their legitimate debts. Judging from the play, Aristophanes regarded the great enlightener as an inimical force, undermining the Athenian credit system. All one-sided economic systems generate anti-intellectualism, and the recent outbreak of fiscal violence against the University of California is an expression of the perduring anti-intellectualism of the United States. Americans want and do not want a college education for their children; they want them tooled up to fit the occupational system but they don't want them enlightened;

and the fiscal blow is the great 'No' citizens of California have bellowed to the question, 'Shall your children be enlightened?'

The United States is not merely another capitalist nation – it is the most powerful one on earth, the power in which corporate profits have the almost abstract quality of light years. In 1965 the sales of the 500 largest American industrial corporations, increasing over previous years, totalled $298 billion. The sales of General Motors alone amounted to $20.7 billion and sixty firms had sales of over a billion dollars. Thus sales for some of these corporations were more than the gross national product of certain Latin American countries. According to *Fortune* magazine, from which these figures are taken, 'Profits for the 500 were fabulous' and were on the rise. General Motors and Standard Oil (New Jersey) each had profits of more than a billion dollars and Ford's was $703 million. Profits on invested capital reached a median of nearly 12 per cent but ranged up to 37·5 per cent.

The American thrust towards limitless wealth and power, meanwhile, has generated not only the reality of anti-intellectualism but also a fearful phantasm. The phantasm – shared by no other developed capitalist power – is the anti-communist nightmare. I do not say that no other capitalist power fears communism; what I do say is that in no other developed capitalist nation has communism become such a nightmare; and the dimension of the phantasm and its hallucinated frightfulness in the United States is in direct proportion to our insatiability. The reason for this is easy to understand; for the greater and the more powerful the thrust towards wealth and power, the greater the real obstacles to it and the greater the imaginary ones also. This is easy for anybody to understand: if I know John Jones does not like me I am not only afraid of him because of what he *does* do to me, but also I magnify in my imagination what he *might* do.

So we have our communist phantasm that the mind of the average frightened American allows no distinction between

Yugoslavia and China, between Norman Thomas, leader of the American socialist party, and Chairman Mao. Since this phantasm adds to fear, it also intensifies anti-intellectualism because it prevents free discussion and penalizes the open-minded.

Starting then, with the fact that the idea of boundless vision has become transformed into insatiability and that insatiability has become institutionalized in the profit system, we see that the idea of man's unlimited potential has made enlightenment next to impossible in my country, because it generates anti-intellectualism. In other words the unlimited turns around and sets limits.

American students have received a great deal of attention in the press lately because they have demonstrated against the war in Vietnam; but their agitation has been directed against the intellectual inadequacy of the American university also. The activity has been exaggerated. You would think, from reading the papers and from listening to many of my colleagues, that the American campus is in ferment from coast to coast. But this is incorrect, for what has come to a boil in Berkeley, California, is almost stone cold in most of the rest of the country. Between the Atlantic and the Pacific Coasts of the United States and from Mexico to Canada, there are vast stretches, spotted with thousands of colleges and universities, where nothing or very little happens from decade to decade, and where student agitation, to the extent that it exists at all, is for better food, removal of curfew, permission to take liquor into the dorms and for more heterosexuality. These are the students who have been so enured to phantasm and to stultified education that they are barely aware that a problem exists. They have nothing to fear because they barely know what there is to fear. Living with phantasm is like living with their own breathing. They are fearless, not because they are brave, but because they are sheep. These are the students who give standing ovations to our war-drum-beating politicians at public ceremonies. These students are the final, self-destructive product of insatiability, anti-intellectualism and phantasm.

Along with these students are the professors who are in the know, but who have learnt to watch their Ps and Qs. There are many of them, but not only in the backwoods and bayou colleges of my country, but also in the universities called great, where for many years important departments, institutes and centres have acted as intellectual barber shops, giving the young just that appearance of smoothness and polish that enables them to play their parts in the anti-enlightenment comedy of American education. A major function of the American educational system is to make social criticism impossible, impolite, and even vulgar.

One of the most interesting aspects of anti-intellectualism in my country is the almost total disappearance of the idea of socialism. In the late nineteenth century, as my colleague, Herbert Gutman, the social historian, has pointed out to me, socialism was a real issue in large sectors of the American labour movement, and the labour newspapers, in attacking the system that was degrading and depriving labour, were not only eloquent and highly literate but full of socialist ideas also. The disappearance of socialism from the American labour papers after the First World War, and the parallel decline in their literary excellence, went hand-in-hand with the rise of the Soviet Union as a world power and the Great Depression. As the Soviet Union grew, both as reality and phantasm, and we emerged frightened from the worst economic collapse in our history, socialism disappeared as a significant ideology from the American scene, ushered out by the American labour movement itself, as it concentrated on wages, working conditions, union stability and fringe benefits. Nowadays American labour never wearies of rushing to assure us that it is lily white.

The result of the disappearance of socialism from the American scene is that there has been no antidote to the phantasm and no counterpoise to the rush to destruction. That is to say, we lack in our country any organized force that might save us from the catastrophe towards which the phantasm is certainly driving us. This is a danger to ourselves and to the rest of the world.

Standing shoulder to shoulder with the red phantasm is its twin, the delusion of invulnerability, for if a people is assailed by a phantasm it can arm itself only with something equally insubstantial. Phantasmic fears call for hallucinatory defences. The mental state came out clearly in the speech of the United States Secretary of Defense Robert McNamara before the American Society of Newspaper Editors on 19 May 1966, when he said that the United States had devoted a higher proportion of its gross national product to its military establishment than any other major free-world nation. He explained that this was true even before the increased expenditure in South-East Asia. Furthermore, for some years past, the US had had as many men in uniform as all the nations of Western Europe combined.

Immense armies, high walls, stables of puppets and satellites, nuclear weapons, shields and umbrellas – all are concrete expressions of the phantasmic fear. Several years ago, when announcing escalation of expenditures for nuclear weapons, a high US Government official explained in a speech the necessity of becoming invulnerable, and averred that such expenditures would indeed make the United States invulnerable. It was a common word in those days in thinking about war. I wrote a letter to the official in which I said that history had shown that there is no such thing as invulnerability, and I received a routine reply. Today, since we confront new Soviet super-defences we are about to try to make ourselves even more invulnerable than before – we are going to try to make what was already unlimited even more so. But even as it becomes apparent, in the limitlessness of space, that there is no invulnerability there, we try to achieve it on land – in Asia and indeed everywhere in the underdeveloped world, by acting as universal gendarme, defending ourselves, and the reluctant world, against phantoms that lie in wait behind each jungle tree and desert dune.

At this point it is necessary to return again to the American economy in order to understand better why we are so self-destructive and destructive of others.

I have pointed out that in the economic sphere limitlessness means aspiration towards boundless profits. Boundless profits can be construed from several points of view; profits as per cent of capital, profits as per cent of sales – how much on each dollar of sales is profit; profits as a totality – that is to say, simply how much profit one makes altogether each year and finally profit as infinitely self-renewing. In the United States the profit *ideal* is a constantly increasing profit *rate* – so that if one year the rate is, let us say, 4 per cent on sales and 15 per cent on capital, the next year it should be 5 and, let us say, 18 per cent respectively. But this ideal cannot be attained in the United States because, although, outside of public utilities there is no legal limit on profits, the structure of the economy is such as to hold profit rates, even of our 500 largest corporations, well below fifty per cent on invested capital. What our industry settles for is total profits – 'fabulous profits', as *Fortune* put it – and profit as a self-renewing force. The fate of the world actually hangs on this decision. The fabulous profits have to be reinvested – they cannot be permitted to pile up in banks; and after investment opportunities have been exhausted at home, the funds, called the *economic surplus*, are invested abroad, for they have no place else to go. But this, in turn, generates new profits, which again have to be invested. Thus American industry becomes a compulsive force pushing towards un-limited acquisition abroad. In this way willy-nilly American capital leaps like a Mephistopheles through the windows of parliaments around the world, and men debate how much Americans shall be permitted to invade their industrial struc-ture. Thus the power of American capital generates a perfectly understandable resistance abroad, but at home this resistance is seen as socialist resistance, wild-eyed Gaullist resistance and so on. The fundamental difference between the United States and all other countries of the world is that it is largely a capital-exporting country. That is to say that, while we do export goods, our capital export – our export of investment funds abroad – so far outruns the export of goods that, relative to the economies of the rest of the world, we are essentially a capital exporting nation. These dollars going abroad for investment must not encounter opposition, for to dam up here would create deflation. In investing abroad, then, we are fleeing from one danger into another; we flee from the *reality* of deflation into the *phantasm* of communism, for we interpret, or let us say, capital interprets, resistance to it now as Red. We have become neurotically hypersensitive to light emanating from the warm end of the spectrum.

This brings me to Vietnam and the history of our involvements in other underdeveloped areas and in Asia since the middle of the last century.

Since 1939[1] the gross national product of the United States has risen steeply, in large part because of the demand for armaments to wage the cold war and to maintain the American universal gendarmerie. A main purpose of this activity has been to keep socialism at bay, and the primary reason for doing so is that socialist economies are useless to a country relying heavily on capital export. Socialist countries will buy abroad, but they want to develop, as far as that is possible, without foreign investment. Our failure to establish more than trivial economic relations with the communist countries no longer derives so much from our reluctance to trade with them as from the fact that we are less interested in trade than in investment.

Meanwhile our military efforts to keep the world free for American investment generate huge economic surpluses, i.e. capital for investment, because the war-nourished industries at home expand the economic surplus. Thus the very process of protecting the world for American investment creates still

1. This section is an abridgement of the author's paper in the *Nation*, 25 April 1966.

greater need for fields in which to invest. The presence of a huge and growing economic surplus makes it absolutely imperative that the world be kept free – for American investment. For that reason we cannot, *under our present system*, ever withdraw our armies from underdeveloped areas, unless we can arrange for a substitute gendarmerie. Corporation profits have no other place to go because the fields for investment at home grow steadily narrower.

Asia represents one of the last frontiers for investment capital. In this connection the following quotes from a Saigon dispatch in the *New York Times* of 12 May 1965 are important:

New industry is developing [in South Vietnam] at an encouraging rate. Moreover, American aid officials believe, several companies operating here for a few years with American financial support are ploughing back their profits into expansion rather than returning them to the United States.

The article then states that the Vietcong have spared industrial developments in South Vietnam, and goes on to say:

In one instance, guerillas made no hostile move against an important dairy products processing plant, backed by American investment, but they attacked a police post only a few hundred yards away.

'When the shooting stops,' a United States aide said, 'there is every expectation of a lively expansion. . .'

American investment in South Vietnamese industry is still light, centred chiefly in three plants: a cotton textile mill, a paper mill, and a dairy products plant. Other companies have surveyed the possibilities and express interest, but are waiting for the situation to improve.

On 9 December 1965 the *New York Times*, in a dispatch from Saigon, revealed that the Bank of America and the Chase National Bank had opened offices in Saigon. The dispatch continues:

Their representatives have quietly visited Saigon in recent weeks for conferences with officials of the National Bank of Vietnam.

At least two other big American financial institutions – the First National City Bank of New York and the American Express Company – are also studying the possibility of opening offices in Vietnam.

Their interest has been whetted by the large number of United States servicemen on duty here. But in the opinion of economic specialists at the American Embassy, Vietnamese businessmen are good potential customers.

The United States, however, is not the only country with banking interests in Vietnam. Ten of the fifteen banks now operating in Saigon are owned by foreigners, particularly by British and French interests. The article continues:

Henry M. Sperry, a First National City Bank vice-president and resident in Hong Kong ... [said] 'We believe we're going to win this war. . . Afterwards, you'll have a major job of reconstruction on your hands. That will take financing, and financing means banks.

'I think the Government here recognizes the need for American banks. It would be illogical to permit the English and the French to monopolize the banking business, because South Vietnam's economy is becoming more and more United States oriented.'

It is clear that investments now being made create a road of no return. Once made, investments must be protected.

The establishment throughout South-East Asia of industrial complexes backed by American capital is sure to have a salutary effect on the development of our foreign involvements: the vast and cheap labour pool will permit competition with the lower production costs of Chinese and Japanese industry, which have immobilized our trading capabilities in Asia for many years.

The history of American involvements in Asia casts light on the foresight of American statesmen. Early in the nineteenth century the British were 'opening doors' in Asia with the simple key of artillery. In 1858 the United States helped open the door of Japan, which at that time was closed to international trade, by sending Admiral Perry to line up an American fleet in Tokyo habour. The Japanese, always quick to accept the inevitable, let the Americans in; but at the same time they launched industrialization and militarization programmes of such power that by the turn of the century Japan had defeated Russia, was rapidly penetrating the Asian market, and was able to squeeze the Americans out. The rest everybody knows: by the 1930s Japan had almost brought China to its knees; it controlled Manchuria and could use China and all of south Asia as outlets for its industrial production. Thus our effort to get into Asia through Japan had boomeranged, and when in 1941 Cordell Hull presented the Japanese with an ultimatum to get out of China, the boomerang hit Pearl Harbor. In short, our economic adventures in Asia helped to embroil us in the Second World War.

After the war Japan – with the help of substantial US orders during the Korean War – became again a world economic power, its growth in recent years being faster than our own (at least until the recent Japanese recession).

Japan must export to live, and China must import to live. Despite American objections trade between Japan and mainland China is expanding. So, having crushed Japan because of its control of China, we assist it to its feet, whereupon it develops trade with China. If the question be asked, 'Who can speak on foreign policy?' one is constrained to answer, 'Surely not the statesmen who planned our past wars; for they lack the power to see beyond their noses.'

Though the dream of the 'co-prosperity sphere' brought Japan to ruin in 1945, news from there suggests that it has not entirely renounced the concept, so that it is clear that if the war in Vietnam ends with victory for the United States, we shall have to confront not only China but also Japan in Asia; for Japan must have Asia as a market – and for the export of *its* surplus capital. Meanwhile Tokyo is intelligently taking advantage of the present American umbrella over South-East Asia, while China is weak and South-East Asia is being 'protected'.

The economic stake of the United States in South-East Asia is presented in a striking way by a full-page ad which Thailand placed in the *New York Times* of 24 January 1966 obviously to attract American investment.

The economic effect of American armed intervention in Asia can be seen in the fact that in that issue of the *Times* South Korea had three full-page advertisements – more than any other country – promoting the country's economic attractions, and calling for foreign investment.

We are fighting in Asia now for the same reason we fought there in the Second World War. In 1941 we told *Japan* to get out of China because Japan had monopolized much of the economic capability of that country. Now we think we are fighting to prevent *China* from monopolizing the economic capability of Asia – including China. Thus we have fought an almost uninterrupted series of wars, beginning with the Second World War, to keep the door in Asia open to American investment. While a military foothold in South-East Asia will permit the expansion of American capital there, an eventual flow of American capital even into China itself is not entirely a pipedream for a far-seeing economics statesman.

If China could be made 'reasonable' it might accept American investment under some form, just as an occasional country in the Russian orbit has accepted foreign investment. Some socialist countries that have excluded foreign capital have found it impossible to get along without it. The removal of Ben Bella in Algeria was followed instantly by broad agreement with France on the exploitation of Algerian oil; and Egypt, after attempting to struggle along without American capital, has at last initiated talks looking to the expansion of American investment there. The economic surplus pleads, then insists, and may eventually use force to gain an outlet; but it never loses patience, for to lose patience is to dam it up at home, and to dam it up is to suffocate the home economy. We would like to keep underdeveloped countries from going socialist but, socialist or not, we want an economic foot in their doors.

Extensive trade by Japan and European countries with mainland China stands in sharp contrast to our fear of the communist dragon. I think the issue is clear: our economic stake in Asia is immense and we cannot turn back because, under present conditions, we need a field of play for our economic surplus, and because we already have an investment to protect in South-East Asia.

Considering the ambiguities and the confusion in Administration statements about Vietnam, and the increasing immensity of our military commitment there, one might conclude that the Administration was mad. But before declaring a man mad, one has to exhaust every clue that bears on his sanity. I think that an examination of our economic situation in Asia makes it clear that the Administration is perfectly sane, as far as sanity goes in such issues, but that it dare not explain its real motives because their revelation would instantly cancel all support for the war. The United States is doing what it has always done: following or attracting the dollar. Our foreign policy has not changed – except in verbiage – since the days of Theodore Roosevelt. In the light of the economic conditions we are literally at bay with China not in the sense that China will swallow South-East Asia physically but in the sense that economic competition with China – and with Japan – is as inevitable as it will be unpleasant. It is clear that we are trying to do in Asia today precisely what we fought Japan for in the Second World War – we are trying to monopolize a market by force of arms.

A final word is necessary about the destruction of the Vietnamese countryside and the disintegration of the peasantry. The history of industry shows that it is impossible to create an industrial revolution without a landless proletariat. The uprooting of peasant life in Vietnam would therefore be preliminary to the industrialization of Vietnam. We know that there is more to rice cultivation than seeds and paddies – it is the *social organization* of the peasantry that makes it possible, the close integration of people in a productive system. The uprooting of families, the killing of the young men, the conversion of the daughters into prostitutes or kept women, the killing of the persons who are repositories of the lore and technique of rice culture, the fall in the birth rate and so on, all make the rehabilitation of the old rice culture impossible and the creation of a landless proletariat inevitable. The uprooted people, however, will find work in the new industrial revolution the war holds miraculously in store for them. There will also be an agricultural revolution, for since the disintegrated peasantry will not be able to farm the land, it will be bought for a song and farmed by 'more modern' methods: large enterprises run by managers and worked by hired hands. The destruction of the Vietnamese countryside would be the first step in the industrialization of Vietnam and the rationalization of its agriculture.

Our war in Vietnam has now reached a climax of barbarism that cannot be justified on any basis. Considering my analysis of how phantasm destroys the possibility of enlightenment, it seems as if, continuing on our present course, we will indeed pass from barbarism to decadence without ever becoming civilized. Meanwhile I am not sure that this has not been the destiny of all so-called high cultures. But before going on to that, I want to give some attention to the efforts in the United States to remove misery at home. For this purpose I shall review briefly President Johnson's sweeping proposals for legislation to improve the conditions of poor children.

On 8 February 1967 he sent a Special Message to Congress on Children and Youth, which contained the following facts and proposals:

In fiscal 1960, the Federal Government invested about $3·5 billion in America's children and youth. In fiscal 1965 that investment rose to $7.3 billion. In fiscal 1968 it will increase to over $11.5 billion – more than three times the amount the Government was spending eight years ago.

This money is to be spent on some of the following projects:

1. Project Head Start: A project to start educating deprived children at the age of three years in order to prepare them to compete better with more privileged children when they enter school. Head Start also will include lunch for needy pre-school children.

2. Establishment of Child and Parent Centres to provide advice and service to parents and children during the pre-natal period and infancy. It would include, among other things, 'day care for children under three years old'.

3. A general programme to train qualified persons to work with children. These would include day care counsellors, parent advisors and health visitors, workers to help children in neighbourhood centres, in health clinics, in playgrounds and in child-welfare agencies. Legislation to raise social security payments to children whose family loses its breadwinner and to increase aid to dependent children of poor families.

4. The president's proposals also include increased expenditures to improve child health, to combat mental retardation and juvenile delinquency, a small pilot project to improve dental care for poor children and a system of summer camps.

The message on Children and Youth is one of several aimed at improving the quality of living in the United States. Thus beside the barbaric external war is an internal enterprise of great scope, not matched by previous administrations. The rest of the world is not much interested in our domestic programmes; but it should be, for knowledge of them might give the world more hope for us. Meanwhile, while we continue to drive the world towards catastrophe and fill it with horror by our war in Vietnam, we can scarcely imagine that what we do at home will interest the world very much. Still it must be pointed out in order that the picture of the United States be more rounded, and in order that we all may understand something more of world history. Regardless of what we were taught in school, it is a fact that all so-called *civilized* nations – from ancient to modern times – have been profoundly barbaric too and *without welfare programmes*. Ancient Athens was built on slavery, war and rapine as well as on trade; the golden age of Spain was a product in part of the barbaric Spanish conquest of the New World; the Italy of Michelangelo had not only its great art but also its savage wars, urban slums and feudal poverty. The glorious literature of England developed side-by-side with imperialistic wars, debtors' prisons, filthy slums, unspeakable poor laws, child labour and so on. While I am horrified by our war in Vietnam, no nation can wrap itself in the mantle of civilization; for, if *civilization be defined as ascendancy of the values of enlightenment, courage, solicitude and universality in the population at large*, it can freely be said that this has never yet been on this earth.

From these considerations of American barbarism and of the immemorial barbarism of mankind, from considerations of insatiability, phantasm, anti-intellectualism and imperialism, I turn away, now, to a more abstract examination of human potentialities within a framework more real than that suggested by the notion of unlimited vision.

I have argued that, though the concept of infinity is useful in mathematics, it is a kind of dangerous hallucination in other human affairs. In other human affairs, I argued, limitlessness is an obsolete idea and belongs on the junkpile of history. Yet, I said, man's intuition of his own limitless possibilities has some basis in fact, and his insatiability is but a corruption of this idea, brought about by boundless disappointment. Thus the idea of unlimited potential is not bad in itself, but becomes so when it is corrupted and transformed by frustration within a corrupt social system.

Early in this address I said that the essence of spirit is an amalgam of courage, solicitude and universality, and it is now time to examine this idea more closely. Courage when applied in the interest of solicitude, and solicitude applied in the interest of the universal, constitute the essence of being what is called a decent human being. Thus in the present state of the world we do not ask for much, and that is a good place to start.

All we ask is that a person have some guts, that he should be very unhappy if other people suffer and that in the exercise of courage and solicitude his vision should extend beyond his family, friends and own country to the rest of the world. What I am saying is that only when vision becomes attached to courage, solicitude and pan-humanness does it have a right to be unlimited. For the average person, the main problem in courage is to know how strong he is – to not exaggerate his own weaknesses or the other person's strength. The principal problem in the evaluation of one's own strength is that we have been taught to think of ourselves as weak, for if we have a really just evaluation of our own power the world cannot do with us what it wants to do. Yet I do not advocate heroics. When I was a boy my father taught me to fight but also imbued me with the idea that he who fights and runs away will live to fight another day. I am not in favour of committing myself to danger, but I am in favour, rather, of knowing the enemy and going ahead or keeping quiet until I am strong. Most people are afraid to criticize anything; they will even roast or freeze to death in a theatre rather than say anything to the usher. A nameless, freezing dread hangs over them. Many will not criticize the government for the same reason. Yet the government of the United States is still remarkably tolerant of dissent and the demonstrations and public outcry against the war are examples.

The greatest value of courage, however, is in protecting others – in solicitude. From the parent who risks his life in order to save his child, to the youth who accepts prison rather than fight a war because he does not want to kill, the courage of solicitude is the true realization of the potential of the soul. And this brings me to the idea of universality. Somewhere along in his education every American child has to memorize Abraham Lincoln's Gettysburg Address. Abraham Lincoln, President of the United States during our Civil War, was one of our great presidents. At Gettysburg, the scene of one of the decisive battles of the Civil War, Lincoln made a famous speech in which he stated that the war was fought in order that 'this nation, of the people, by the people and for the people, shall not perish from the earth'. Nowadays, however, no nation can be only for its own people, and no war, not even civil wars, are fought in isolation, for even a civil war like the one for example, in the Congo, is related to a nation's international involvements and has international repercussions. Hence the importance of universality and hence the importance of universality as a central ingredient of the soul.

10. Social and Psychological Preparation for War*

War is fought by social groups. Social groups exist in a mobilized and unmobilized condition. For the conduct of everyday affairs social groups are integrated, tied together, by processes which, ranging from the simple exchange of commodities and services of tribal peoples, to the interlocking corporations, fiscal obligations and controls and industry – government relations in modern states, provide continuity and dependability. Mobilized, such groups are prepared for extra effort, for an output greater than the requirements of everyday life. In time of war latent capabilities for action are actualized, with the aid of the society's capacity for love, hate and anxiety.

Defining the Enemy. The 'enemy', however, is, himself, an aspect or mode of the dialectics of the organization of the society. In the tribal world, for example, where, as compared with the modern world, each society is relatively self-contained, the 'enemy' is usually outside the social system.[1]

In the modern world, however, the enemy is, by definition, and by dialectic necessity, a part, but also not a part, of the

* Reprinted from David Cooper (ed.), *The Dialectics of Liberation* (London, 1968).

1. The Indian tribes of eastern South America constitute an outstanding exception to this generalization. For one example see my *Jungle People* (New York, 1965 – first published in 1941).

'friendly' social configuration that acts against it in war. In modern states the 'enemy' is linked to one's own social system by trade, by various cultural ties, by diplomatic relations, and so on, as well as by destructive chains of impulses and activities. The initial bellicose step of 'breaking relations' testifies to this ambiguity. The requirement in modern warfare that the enemy usually be part of the social system of the contending countries and, at the same time, not part, is one of the social inventions of modern civilization, for if one goes back to ancient histories one perceives that ancient wars were often, though not always, fought against enemies not part of one's social system. The enemies of ancient Greece and Rome were often mere objects of their imperial arrogance and rapine, having no previous social relations with Greece and Rome. Thus one of the 'achievements' of the modern world is to incorporate war directly into the social system, while defining the enemy as outside it. The net consequence of this, for the United States, has been sundry Marshall Plans, foreign-aid programmes, economic development plans for South-East Asia, and the like. These programmes recognize the essentially *internal* nature of modern war and modern enemies. The post-war 'compassion' of the modern 'victor', which recognizes the basic unity of the world social system, and therefore dresses the enemy's wounds, is at 180 degrees from those ancient wars, in which the defeated enemy was put to the sword, enslaved, or condemned to tribute. This modern 'compassion' is partly a consequence of interlocking international corporations, partly an expression of the need to use one's former enemies against one's former friends. America's use of Japan – particularly of Okinawa – as a staging area and source of supply for the war in Vietnam, and her support of German claims and hopes against the Soviet Union, are cases in point.

A basic fact of modern warfare, then, is that it occurs within a mutually dependent world political economy and that all victories are therefore defeats for the people – for they have borne the burden of death and, through taxation, must bear the economic burden of compassion – and victories for the vanquished, for they often see their economies beautifully reconstructed. Japan is an excellent case in point.[2] Nowadays Japanese capital competes with American almost everywhere in the world, Japan is almost as deeply involved as the United States in Canada, and Japan has heavy investments in Alaska. Indeed Japan's economic fate is so closely linked to that of the United States that on 9 February 1967, when rumours of peace in Vietnam broke out, prices for 225 selected stocks on the Tokyo market dropped an average of 42.12 points, the worst setback since 19 July 1963.[3]

To continue with the example of Japan, business and technological know-how combined with low wages have given Japan such economic power that US involvement in South-East Asia is aimed as much at monopolizing that market against Japanese penetration as against Chinese. The Vietnam War is indirectly a war against Japan, who is part of our social system, and whom, at the same time, the US is using in order to further her ends in Asia.

Not all wars are shooting wars or even cold ones. For years the United States has been fighting a kind of cold war with France, and England is a kind of casualty of that war. France's (largely unsuccessful) efforts to keep American capital out, its determination to build its own computer industry and nuclear capability, its efforts to diminish American gold paramountcy and its objection to Britain's entrance into the Common Market are all expressions, in part, of fear of United States' economic power. The contemporary world system, even when it is 'friendly', constantly defines internal enemies. It is a system in which there is no guarantee that, at any moment, the poker

2. Japan's gross national product in the 1960s is many times what it was before the Second World War. See *Newsweek: Economic Almanac 1964* and *Japan: Statistical Yearbook 1965.*

3. *New York Times,* 2 October 1967.

players sitting around an amicable table, as in an American Western, might not pull a gun or five aces.

It is clear therefore that in preparation for modern war an interdependent world political economy has within it sufficient conflicts of interest to make all nations potential enemies to all others. One of the 'evolutionary achievements' of modern culture has been to make the idea that 'anybody can be my enemy at any time' acceptable. A consequence of the definition of the enemy as part of one's own social system is a psychological predisposition to accept almost any nation at all as inimical when the government chooses to so define it.

While it is true that the present organization of the world makes all nations potential enemies to one another, the absolute division of the world into communist and non-communist nations multiplies the probability of enemies. Here we must ask: who divides the world into communist and non-communist? And the answer is, of course, those who stand to gain by it. Obviously the John Does did not make the division; and obviously the example of Western Europe in 1967 suggests that the *perception* of that division as rigidly constituting the very *essence* of the modern world is not universal. Though it is true that the countries of Eastern Europe are roughly 'communist', they have different forms of communism, and in some sense, one could hardly say that Yugoslavia could be called communist at all. Meanwhile, however, the *perception* of these nations by others varies also, so that though Americans see them all as inimical, Europeans perceive them less nightmarishly. The point at issue is that the social organization of the world has no essence. The delusion that is made to appear as essence is manufactured by those who stand to gain by it and it is burned into the minds of the population by the media, which are, of course, controlled by the same people. This delusion then takes on the character of a true perception of the world, seeming as absolute to the average man as the difference between red and green.

In the United States the world is simplistically perceived by most people as made up of communist and 'free' nations, and all the former are perceived as enemy – as the enemies of 'freedom'. This simplistic definition of the world, however, is not accepted by much of Western Europe and the United Kingdom. The definition is thus a parochial American one, based on the interests of those who foster it. If the French do not perceive the world as Americans do, it is because French interests have nothing to gain by it but much to lose. The condition of West Germany, meanwhile, is absurd because, on the one hand, corporate interests there have everything to gain by forgetting the 'communist-free world' definition and division, while, on the other, no West German government could risk American pressure or a victory of the extreme right by seeming to cancel the old feud with the Soviet Union. American interests can only be furthered by German hankerings after old borders, for they help maintain the USSR in a state of expensive alert.

No Options. The present situation in the Near East makes it clear that the organization of the world offers mankind limited options. When we consider that *shalom*, peace, is the word with which ordinary Israelis greet one another, that they are a people who know, better than most perhaps, what war means and that only through incredible toil and peace have they been able to create a home in the desert, their war with the Arab states seems an unbelievable contradiction. Yet the configuration of the world society, of which they are part, and the fact that the world system defined them as another enemy within, inexorably drove them to war. The social structure of the modern world has so limited the possibilities of existence that even emerging nations from whom we might expect some new ideas, some new salvation, are forced, often against their will, into the old ways of predator and prey. North Vietnam and the Congo are further examples of emerging nations forced into an old pattern. The present world political economy leaves mankind almost no room to exploit or to think about new ways of political existence. This means that under the present system man has no choice but to make war upon himself. It means then either that Nature intends Man to become extinct, or that She is compelling him to devise a new system.

The social preparation for modern war therefore involves the following steps: 1. Establishment of a world system in which betrayal, conspiracy and entrapment are so commonplace that at any moment whoever is within the friendly system may be defined as outside of it; so commonplace, indeed, that people accept it without thinking. 2. Manipulation of that system solely in the interests of particular classes or groups who stand to gain by particular definitions. 3. The manipulation, the moulding of the perceptual capacities of the people by these groups through their control of the mass media. 4. The establishment of a world-wide social system which strictly limits choice in the solution of problems. In this context, Charles de Gaulle's efforts to free France of American economic entanglements represent not only an effort to be free of the United States as such, but also an effort to be free of limiting options; to be free to seek new solutions to the problems of a hampering social system; and in this context English economic entanglement with the United States illustrates the impossibility of ever arriving at new solutions to one's problems as long as one is committed to a powerful ally who sees only the old, and limited, possibilities. The same holds within the group of states allied to the USSR. I hope I am making myself clear. All social systems have been set up in such a way as to limit options. Whether it be a primitive tribe where a man must marry his mother's brother's daughter and cultivate his land with the help of his clan brothers only; whether it be the members of the old British Commonwealth, trading largely with those within the sterling area; or whether it be the United States government trying to stop the sale by other nations of so-called strategic materials to the 'communist' nations, every society, throughout history, has buttressed its internal structure

and mobilized against outsiders by limiting choice. Fundamentally, primordially, free choice has been viewed as inimical to any
social system. Arguments about free choice, therefore, have
been absurd when they have not been hypocritical.

The American Economy

I turn now to an analysis of the organization of the American
economy: In order to show how readily it can be mobilized for
anything at all.

In order that any social system be mobilized for war, which
means mobilization for maximum effort, it must have forms of
structure – institutions – which can swiftly be brought together
and integrated into a war system when necessary. While it might
appear 'only natural' that America should have been able to
produce the implements of war that made victory over the Axis
possible, the astonishing and rapid organization of that productive capability was not accomplished easily, nor was it accomplished just before or during the Second World War. The latent
possibility for such organization – its infrastructure – existed
long before the Second World War, and the consolidation
process was hastened by the immense insecurity of the Great
Depression. 'The modern centralized, militarized, and welfare-
directed state'[4] is the result of a complex internal evolution
taking several decades. I shall trace the pattern.

Concentration and Size. The ability of any social unit to wage war
or indeed to exercise power in any way is a function of its size,
of the resources it controls and of its organization. In this connection we have to understand something of the dimensions of
the larger American corporations. In 1962 the four largest

4. These are the words of Thomas C. Cochran in his book *The American
Business System* (Cambridge, Mass., 1960), p. vii. Dr Cochran is Professor
of American History at the University of Pennsylvania.

automobile manufacturers accounted for nearly 80 per cent of the automobile sales in the United States; the two largest steel companies for 30 per cent of the sales and the ten largest oil companies accounted for more than 85 per cent of the petroleum refining and related industry sales. Twenty-eight of the largest industrial and commercial companies accounted for almost a quarter of the sales of the manufacturing companies in the United States.[5]

The United States Steel Corporation, which in 1965 produced one quarter of the total steel output of the United States,[6] is an integrated corporation, which owns and operates not only numerous steel producing and fabricating plants, but also iron and coal mines, limestone quarries, railways, docks, cargo vessels and loading ships. Through several score plants in the United States it manufactures thousands of products, ranging from cold rolled steel to prefabricated housing, cement, ordnance, atomic energy products, components and launching facilities for nuclear missiles, armour plate, etc., etc., etc.[7] The size of the corporation, however, is not measured only by the plants directly connected with it, but includes also its seventeen subsidiaries through which it controls raw materials, railroads and other transportation facilities in Canada, Brazil, Venezuela, Africa and the Bahama Islands. Through its management and board of directors the influence of US Steel, meanwhile, extends far beyond its plants and subsidiaries. In 1962 its eighteen directors accounted for eighty-five management interlocks with other companies, over which these directors might be expected to exercise influence, and these interlocks included twenty banks and financial institutions, ten insurance companies and fifty-four industrial-commercial corporations. Thus Mr C. H. Bell, for

5. p. 115 of 'Interlocks in Corporate Management', a Staff Report of the Antitrust Subcommittee (Subcommittee Report No. 5) of the Committee on the Judiciary, US House of Representatives, 12 March 1965.

6. *Moody's Manual 1966*, p. 2230.

7. *Moody's Manual 1966*, pp. 2229–32.

example, was also a director of General Mills Inc., the Winton Lumber Company and the Northern Pacific Railway; and Mr J. B. Black sat on the board of directors of FMC corporation, Del Monte Properties Company, Pacific Gas and Electric Company, Southern Pacific Company, Shell Oil, Pacific Gas Transmission Company, Alberta Natural Gas Company and the Alberta and Southern Gas Company Ltd.[8]

The Dow Chemical Company,[9] manufacturer extraordinary of napalm and explosives, operates several dozen plants in the United States, but through subsidiaries and through part ownership it controls or is deeply involved in other scores of manufacturing operations and corporations in the United Kingdom (Dow Chemical International Ltd), Switzerland, the Netherlands, Germany, Australia, India and Spain. Through its affiliation with Schlumberger Ltd, Dow substantially controls plants in France, Germany, Spain, Spanish Sahara, Algeria, Libya, Tunisia, Iran, Venezuela, Trinidad, Bolivia and Argentina. Other operations substantially controlled by Dow are in Japan (Asahi-Dow Ltd) and Ecuador. Literally the sun never sets on Dow! Thus through sheer size, through subsidiaries, through ownership of stock in other corporations and through management interlocks, the large American corporations control much of the productive capability of the planet. In 1951, 135 American corporations *owned* nearly a fourth of the manufacturing volume of the world.[10] This says nothing about how much is *controlled*, how much is a sphere of interest, that is not owned outright.

The presence of hundreds of corporations, which, in their day-to-day operations, can, through their social organization,

8. 'Interlocks . . .', pp. 126–8.

9. *Moody's Manual 1966*, pp. 2804–5.

10. 'The Measurement of Industrial Concentration' by M. A. Adelman, in *The Review of Economics and Statistics*, Vol. XXX, No. 2, 1951. Quoted in A. A. Berle, Jr, *The 20th Century Capitalist Revolution* (New York, 1954).

call upon such an immensely ramifying network of productive power, provides the United States with a vast war potential.

Interest Groups. The internal organization of the companies themselves, plus their interlocks, does not of itself constitute the social organization of American corporate power. These great masses of capital are further organized in what has been called 'interest groups'.[11] The interest group is a group of corporate interests which, through interlocking directorates, mutual stock ownership, financial support, auditing and legal activities and membership in the same trade organizations, come to pursue common financial goals. If various companies share board members and own one another's stocks and bonds; if, further, certain financial institutions assume the burden of underwriting (financial responsibility) and disposing of stock flotations for certain corporations, while others consistently render legal and auditing services to all, we have a common financial interest and therefore a common-interest group. *The Structure of the American Economy* lists *eight* such groups: 1. The Morgan-First National, 2. Rockefeller, 3. Kuhn, Loeb, 4. Mellon, 5. Chicago, 6. Du Pont, 7. Cleveland, 8. Boston.

I present an abbreviated account of one such group, the Morgan-First National, as it stood on the last date for which we have adequate information. *The Structure of the American Economy* states that

This group is for the most part based upon partial control by one or the other, or, more commonly, by both of the financial institutions (i.e. J. P. Morgan & Company and The First National Bank) after which the group is named. This partial control is based upon long-standing financial relations and the very great prestige attaching to the Morgan and First National firms . . .

11. In *The Structure of the American Economy* (Washington, 1939). While some of the data in this great book are out of date, the main features of the analysis remain substantially correct.

When that passage was written, the group included thirteen industrial corporations, thirteen public-utilities corporations, six railway systems and three banks besides Morgan and First National. In 1939, the last date for which we have these figures, their total assets were more than thirty billion dollars.

But this is not the end of this pyramiding of power, for the interrelationships among the interest groups themselves result in further concentration and integration. Thus there are close relations through interlocking directorates, underwriting, mutual stock ownership and so on between Morgan-First National and Mellon; between Morgan-First National and Chicago; between Kuhn, Loeb and Cleveland, and so on. Altogether, from the eight basic interest groups there emerge eleven overlaps. At the end of their analysis of interest groups, the authors of *The Structure of the American Economy* ask the following questions, which they do not answer:

What is the significance of the existence of more or less closely integrated interest groups for the pricing process? What are its implications for the relation between economic and political activity? How and to what extent do the views of leaders in the economic sphere make themselves felt in the life of the community?

These questions were not put by Marxists, for the committee that prepared the study was made up of six members of President Franklin D. Roosevelt's cabinet and four experts highly placed in American government and business. At any rate, it is clear that this is an organization 'in being', which, once mobilized by government, can exert irresistible power for war – or for peace. *It has never been mobilized for peace.*

The structure of *corporate* controls in the American economy has been set forth. What is still missing, what still remains to be elucidated is what makes it possible for government to use this organization for its own purposes when necessary; or, rather, for them to use each other.

·   ·   ·   ·   ·

Relationships between Government and Business. The most important relationship between business and government in the United States, or, rather, the reliance of the corporate community on government, began to take its present form during the Great Depression. Previously it was believed that the capitalist system was self-regulating, and this view, voiced by economists, was echoed, with certain embroidery of intonation and syllable, by famous sociologists like Pareto in Italy and by Talcott Parsons, Professor of Sociology at Harvard University, in the United States. It is important to bear in mind the connections between the illusions of the economists and those of the sociologists. Before the Great Depression nearly overturned the capitalist system in the United States, it was believed that depressions were somehow an expression of the inexorable operation of an eternal system and that depressions always worked themselves out spontaneously. Depressions, it was believed, were nature's way of eliminating inefficient and weak firms, while leaving the field to strong, 'parent', companies, able to beget powerful off-spring. The Depression, however, saw so many of the strong fail and threatened so many of the strongest, as month after month, year after year, the economy did not recover, while more and more businesses failed, and twenty-five per cent of the American labour force was unemployed, that the corporate community was happy to seize the hand of government when it was extended in help. It was this *vulnerability* that created the new 'government-underwritten society' in the United States; but which also served to mobilize the United States better than ever for war. It was primarily the threat of internal collapse that perfected the underlying structure of mobilization for war; and it is clear that without such mobilization the economy would have collapsed. As late as 1940, when the United States was starting to arm, a conservative estimate of the number of unemployed in the American labour force was 13 per cent, but by 1944 they had all been put to work and the total number of employed workers had increased by 35 per cent.[12] During the Depression, however, new legislation enabled labour to organize at a tremendous rate and the Second World War gave the American workers an unprecedented rise in living standard. Organized labour was brought into wartime government, and the Office of Production Management was headed jointly by William S. Knudsen of General Motors and Sidney Hillman of the Amalgamated Clothing Workers, a powerful, but rather conservative member of the Congress of Industrial Workers. The experience of the Second World War was not lost on the American labour movement: war meant jobs, plenty of money and good times. Today organized labour in the United States is an active supporter of the war in Vietnam; and it is among the most virulent internal antagonists of the Soviet Union.

Industry and the Military. Since 1939 immense US Government expenditures for armaments, and, more recently, for space exploration, have increased the power of the great corporations and created many new businesses. The aircraft industry is largely dependent on orders for military aircraft. The entrance of numerous business executives into government service during the Second World War consolidated the intimate relationship between government and business. But the end of the consolidation was not yet in sight. What was needed was a marriage of the military to industry. Considering the fact that most of the national budget of the United States now goes for military purposes, it was only natural that upon leaving the armed forces, or the Department of Defense, military men should be eagerly sought as employees and members of boards of directors by business.

In July 1960 . . . General Dynamics, the corporation having the largest per cent of armaments contracts (by dollars), had 27 retired generals and admirals on its payrolls. The *total* number of retired

12. *The American Business System*, p. 134.

officers of all ranks employed by General Dynamics, however, was about 200. Its closest competitor was United Aircraft, with 171.[13]

All figures are probably low estimates. Meanwhile we should not forget, of course, that Mr Robert McNamara, former president of the Ford Motor Company, is our Secretary of Defense and that an earlier one was Charles Wilson, President of General Motors.

I have outlined the organization of American industry that provides the social infrastructure for war. I have shown that the basis is in the first place the giant corporation with its ramifying network of plants, subsidiaries and stock-holdings that extend its influence throughout the nation and the world. I then pointed out how these corporations are linked to one another and organized into interest groups which are interlocked among themselves. I then described the process whereby the American corporate community, abandoning for ever the cry against government interference, became amalgamated with government, and I pointed out how the military has become part and parcel of American business. Given this structure, the traditional division of our society into business, government and military seems obsolete and illusory. Given this structure it is possible to mobilize American industry for maximal war output almost instantaneously. It is not far-fetched to say that now, *by its very nature it is in a constant state of mobilization for war*.

Psychological Factors

Vulnerability. While it is true that in all ages man has felt vulnerable, it is worth while to examine certain of the aspects of the feeling of vulnerability in the United States in order to understand how it contributes to readiness for war. I have pointed out that before the Great Depression it was assumed that the capitalist economy was self-regulating but that the depression

13. Quoted from my *Culture against Man*, p. 105.

experience destroyed that idea for ever in the minds of even the most bumptious economists, so that now all the 'talented' men of capitalist economics take the Keynesian theory of necessary government economic intervention for granted and instantly propose government measures whenever the economy seems to falter – which is now several times a year. The ordinary American, however, does not yet feel that the economy is to be trusted for it has an unpredictable way of raising prices on him, throwing him out of a job or making his little investments and speculations vanish. The feeling of vulnerability in the United States is intensified by the increase in the number and power of socialist countries and by the fact that, since the government–business–military complex cannot accept this as a tolerable fact of existence, they frighten the people.

The emergence since 1917 of this new socialist humanity has been accompanied by the disappearance or weakening of many capitalist powers, to the degree that, feeling beleaguered amidst the diminished strength of the capitalist world, America, according to Secretary of Defense Robert McNamara,

has devoted a higher proportion of its gross national product to its military establishment than any other free-world nation. This was true even before the increased expenditures in South-East Asia.

We have had, over the last few years, as many men in uniform as all the nations of Western Europe combined – even though they have a population half again greater than our own.[14]

The rise of socialism and the doubling of the number of violent revolutions since 1958 (also according to Mr McNamara) left the American corporate community feeling so vulnerable that it eagerly and successfully communicated its fear and hate to the American people through the mass media. The result has been, as everyone knows, a supine Congress and a public that gives

14. Address to the American Society of Newspaper Editors, as reported in the *New York Times*, 19 May 1966.

support to whatever the American government desires to do any place in the world.

Terror and Euphoria. In the economic view there are fundamentally two types of consumption, consumption in the private and consumption in the public sectors of the economy. Consumption in the private sector refers to egoistic things – all that a person buys to make living possible and enjoyable – but extending also to business expenditures; while consumption in the public sector refers to things like roads, schools, armaments and so on, on which government spends money. All governments have to calculate how much can be exacted in taxes for consumption in the public sector, while the need for the taxes is sold to the people by a combination of public relations, scaring and coercion. Taxes to support the war in Vietnam are exacted through scaring Americans with communism. Although taxes for government expenditures generally compete with spending for egoistic satisfactions, the American system of taxation converts exactions for public expenditures into egoistic consumption because taxes return to the consumer through the higher wages, higher employment and elevated standard of living that result from the pouring of hundreds of billions of dollars into war industry. Since in the United States corporations and the rich are taxed most, and taxes are not permitted to rise faster than real income, the average John Doe finds himself better off during war. Thus the government, primarily through war and the graduated income-tax system and capital-gains taxes, has produced such domestic euphoria that its public expenditures – primarily its expenditures for war and space – have the psychological effect of egoistic ones. Since it is fear – fear of communism – that makes Americans willing to pay the taxes for armaments in the first place, but since these taxes come back to them in good living, we can say that literally Americans grow fat on fear. What fear they might have of war is narcotized by good times. When we consider that, in view of Vietnam, the

Russians have had to slow down expansion in the production of consumer goods in order to put more effort into the production of armaments, we see that one traditional psychological obstacle to war does not exist for Americans.

Confusion between Friend and Enemy. During the Second World War Japan was our enemy, now she is our friend; the Soviet Union was our friend, now she is our enemy; Germany was our enemy, now part of her is friend, part enemy; France was our friend, now she is almost our enemy; Yugoslavia was our friend, now she is our friend one day, our enemy the next, as our foreign policy shifts. During the Second World War China was our friend, now she is our enemy. Before the war in the Middle East we were able to live comfortably with our anti-semitism, now we see our government incomprehensibly on Israel's side; during the Second World War Italy was our enemy, now she is our friend – and so it goes. In the ordinary citizen the result of these wild fluctuations in the definition of enemy and friend can only be mental withdrawal, cynicism and a readiness to resign decisions to 'higher powers' and 'experts'. On the other hand such passivity in the presence of radical alterations in the definition of the enemy could take place only if we had handed over decisions to higher powers in the first place. The American's lack of involvement in anything but his standard of living and his family, plus a persisting feeling of vulnerability, make him accept easily any alteration in foreign policy. Meanwhile I doubt that in this Americans are much different from the rest of the world called civilized.

In this connection we see the importance of short-run perceptions. It is as if modern man never committed his perceptual apparatus permanently to any definition. It is disquietingly like the perception of style. Style depends on short-run perceptions; on the fact, for example, that though a dark tie may seem best with one's suit today, there is always present in the mind the reservation that this is not for ever, but only as long as some power defines it as style. I find something similar in the academic world. There is, for example, no commitment in anthropology or sociology to any point of view. Acceptance of contemporary theorists lasts, at the most, just about as long as they are alive. When they die, no one quotes them any more. Sometimes a theory lasts only a semester. While I do not consider acceptance or rejection of a foreign power homologous with style or with acceptance of a social theory, I do believe that all three rely on a condition of contemporary perception – the withholding of commitment to any view of the world. This superficiality, this fundamental impenetrability of the soul, is due to the evanescent quality of modern life and to the basic depression of modern man.

The Inimical Factor in Life. A culture has never been found where there was not a permanent inimical factor that served to terrify and to integrate the people and to suffocate deviant opinion. In tribal life the inimical beings are monsters or spirits and outside enemies, defined by tradition as everlastingly dangerous to mankind or to the tribe or both. One is trained from infancy to accept these inimical ones as eternal and unchanging, and no one says they do not exist or that they are friendly or that their friendship can be won. The threat of the inimical stifles thought but also creates social solidarity.

In the contemporary world, as contrasted with the tribal, the inimical lacks *traditional* definition, and the group in power reserves to itself the right, and the power, to define who and what the inimical shall be. The definition then becomes part of the social system: lessons about the inimical are taught to elementary-school children; the mass media scream its name with appropriate invective; the inimical becomes part of the legal system and it becomes incorporated into the economic framework. It becomes as inexorable as a primitive hallucination, and doubting it carries the same punitive social consequences. In the United States the inimical is communism.

Incorporated into elementary-school readers and sociological tracts, frozen into supreme-court decisions and loyalty oaths, and consolidated further through embargoes on goods to communist countries, the communist bogy has the qualities of a tribal delusion. The delusion of the 'communist menace' represents the exploitation of man's primordial tendency to define some part of the universe as inimical, in order to prepare the American people for war.

Freedom, Enterprise and Docility. When we consider the international structure of the American corporate community and the fact that the sun never sets on it, it is clear that 'free world' means the part of it that is free for American investment. It is for that reason that Spain, for example, is considered part of the 'free world'. On the other hand, when we realize that there is no owned American investment in communist countries, we comprehend why the communist world is not 'free'. Yet, when we know that the United States supplies heavy machinery which Italy is using in its Fiat installation in the Soviet Union, we understand, in part, why Russia seems 'freer' to us now than it used to be.

Americans are used to the expression 'free enterprise', yet it is clear from the outline of the structure of the American economy that the expression has no meaning at all. The tightly woven fabric of the American economy leaves little room for 'enterprise', and over the past several decades the type of person heading up large corporations has changed from the individual master builder to the long-time-serving, loyal and cautious executive, who is guided by his board of directors, underwriters, accounting and legal firms and research department. Nowadays corporations rarely fire anybody, even at the lower levels; as long as they are docile and fit the over-all gentlemanly pattern of operations, they are moved around in the firm until they find a niche. Decisions are very much by committee and not by individuals. All of this is well known and has been popularized in a penetrating book by William H. White, Jr, called *The Organization Man.*

Similar processes are at work in labour. The ideal American labour leader nowadays is not a daring man who risks injury or death in a strike, but a careful negotiator, who is backed by a team of lawyers and researchers. The labour movement in the United States nowadays is very different from what management confronted in the 1920s, armed for deadly combat. Organized labour is probably the most contented segment of the American population; it has shifted from being the most revolutionary group to being the most conservative.

Along with these alterations in the structure of American political economy there has developed a vast, sheep-like docility in the population. Grazing on the grasses of affluence, the white American population is one of the most docile on earth. This is ideal psychological preparation for war, for docile people make excellent soldiers.

Let me summarize what I have said up to this point about the psychological factors that prepare for war. I have said that feeling vulnerable we are ever on the defensive. TV shows, for adults or for children, that portray individuals and nations under attack are the commonest programme. Meanwhile, as we are frightened into paying heavy taxes to 'save' ourselves and support our wars, we have a wonderful time, for taxes come back to us in increased income. So Americans grow fat on their fear and fear feels good, or, at least, better than it ever did before. It is hard to be against the war in Vietnam if your pay has gone up because of it. I referred to American docility and the readiness to accept as friend the nation that was a foe yesterday and to accept as enemy today the nation that was a friend yesterday. Since in the United States one is never threatened really by such erratic definitions, but finds rather that one's standard of living rises, why object? It is a law of learning theory that organisms tend to respond positively to a stimulus that is rewarding. In the American experience having enemies has been rewarding. The fact that some people have lost sons is of little consequence, for the personal detachment, withdrawal and uninvolvement of the American, his inability to feel for another person's bereavement, his concern only with what is close to him and with his standard of living, make him impervious to the sorrow of others. Furthermore, as I pointed out, the depressive core in the soul of the American population makes people turn away from the anguish of others, while brooding only on their own. I spoke, then, of the inimical factor in life, of the fact that in the modern, as contrasted with the tribal, world, the inimical is selected by the group in power and of the fact that the perceptual functions of the people are shaped to suit this group's objectives. In modern times perception has rapidly evolved away from tradition-determined perceptions of the world to class-determined ones and perception is manipulated by the mass media. So one acquires and puts off one's enemies and friends, one's ideas, one's opinions, and one's tastes somewhat as one changes style. Finally I pointed out the lack of sense in the words 'freedom' and 'enterprise'. The last point I take up is the psychological consequences of the disappearance from life of any real options, of any real freedom.

No Exit.[15] It is clear that freedom exists only where there are real options; where the individual, or a nation, in spite of its history, can make a choice that is not over-determined by the system. While it is unlikely that at any time man's choices were *not* over-determined; while it is unlikely that *Homo sapiens* ever had a local or international system that allowed him to invent new solutions to his old problems, I feel that never before have so many felt that they lived in a room with no exit. This results in apathy and withdrawal from life. Meanwhile the attractiveness of withdrawal is enhanced by the high-rising standard of living and the increased possibilities for good times, which

15. The last section of my paper takes its title from Sartre's famous play.

narcotize all feeling, and by the extreme danger of going against the multitude. The knowledge that there are no options, the feeling of entrapment, the feeling that one can do nothing because there are no doors, makes its inevitable contribution to war; for not only does it lead to ready acceptance of war as a solution to difficult problems, but it creates docility also. Man is everywhere chained to a system in which he perceives no new options. Yet there are – for the vast and radical political changes that have occurred in the past two generations prove that man can create new options where there seemed to be none.

11. Cross-Cultural Education

The expression 'cross-cultural' refers to communication between cultures or a comparison of different cultures. I shall explain by examples from my own experience. I had scarcely been among the Kaingáng Indians of Brazil for more than a few days, when they held a ceremony. I camped on the ceremonial ground, and, following what I thought was good field method, gave presents to Indians who did me a kindness. I quickly discovered that, having got the idea that I would give a present for whatever was done for me, the Indians were manufacturing entirely unnecessary favours – that I was swamped with solicitude I did not need. I had educated them to perform unwanted tasks by not making the issue clear, and I had to announce that I was giving no more presents. The favours ceased. On the last day of the ceremony, when the Indians were drunk, they decided that I ought to give away all the trade goods I had brought with me to the ceremony. They therefore gathered around me, drunk and smelling of honey-beer, and demanded that I hand them over. Some Indians were carrying lances and others were armed in other ways, and it seemed to me that there was some question of intimidation, although I believe now that that was not really in their minds. At any rate, surrounded by such apparent determination, I might have given in and handed over everything I had. Yet I reasoned that if I yielded they would get the idea that all they had to do to get me to give up what I had was to make some show of force; in that case I would not be able to keep anything. But I reasoned also that if I talked long enough something might happen; so I kept talking. I still talked only Portuguese, so what was said between us had to be translated by the few who knew that language. The shadows of the great trees were already beginning to make night in that clearing and I was still talking, when an Indian suggested that if I gave them something they would give me something. This was the break I was waiting for and I at once consented, promising to give each man, woman and child something if they gave me the objects – drinking troughs, rattles, ornaments, etc. – they had used in the ceremony. This was the core of the collection I took back with me to the United States. The suggestion was an excellent example of communication between cultures.

Before settling on the reserve fifteen years previous to my coming, the Kaingáng, armed with bow, lance and club, practically naked, and sleeping in hastily built huts in the rainy season, had been ferocious killers, hunted and hunting. Nevertheless they shared all their food and property freely with one another and would stand by one another to the death. Even when I was there, all favours were freely given and all property freely taken. They had no conception of payment nor of accumulation. Whatever one had was simply given away or appropriated by a relative without asking. To store accumulations such as I and other white men had was foreign to them. It is therefore clear why they were intoxicated with my property and found the whole idea of being paid for merely doing something for somebody so exotic that they exploited it. Furthermore, since they were very poor in our terms, whatever I gave, no matter how trivial, was a real acquisition. At the ceremony they became drunk with something more than the beer – it was the idea of so much property. What is necessary is to search out exactly what it is that has stimulated the other person. It cannot be taken for granted; one is often wrong.

I think we can now come to grips with the problem of cross-cultural education. Kaingáng culture was different from mine because we followed very different ways of life. Since we were strangers, communication was halting. It was a long time before I understood their ideas of property, but, when I did, communication could be said to have taken place across the cultures – from the members of one culture to a member of another culture. But it took me many months to learn the exact nature of the mistake I had made; and, of course, they didn't care. They had no cultivated intermediary to educate me to their ways – I had to labour to learn them. The education across cultures was *their* education of me. I think I educated them in a different way: by holding on to most of what I had, I convinced them that I was just another stingy white man; or as they called us, *thugng*, which means enemy. In the course of my stay I tried to adapt to their way, but obviously I could not really, for if I had given away everything, as they wished me to, I would not have been able to trade. I was stuck in my notion of trading, unable to understand, that if I gave away everything I had to them, I would then have a right to take from them what I wanted without asking, which is what they did with one another. So, although I came to understand their mode, I could not free myself of my own – I was marooned in my rigidity. So I remained always on the outside, though I learned their language and treated their illnesses and injuries free. They came to have splinters taken out of their feet, to have their legs, ulcerated by constant collisions with thorns and fallen logs, bandaged; when they all came down with the flu I doctored them; treated them for intestinal parasites, and so on. Thus the white man understands, in terms of his culture, that healing the sick is a grace and should be done free to the lower orders and when it is to his advantage. That understanding made a different kind of communication possible; and the Kaingáng were educated by me to understand that some *thugng*, though miserly with one kind of property, are free with another.

Though the Kaingáng had roamed untrammelled in the tropical rain forest, never remaining for more than a week in one place, hunting the tapir, the deer, the coati, the peccary and wild birds, when they settled on the reserve they became part time farmers. Since they were poor, however, and I had a supply of implements, they would come to borrow mine, and I lent them freely, always, however, asking for a few handfuls of beans, a few ears of corn in return. But the Kaingáng never brought anything, for they had no concept of repayment, they fed only their own, feeding was based on need and I had more than enough. So I never collected those minimal token repayments, which seemed so necessary to my American conscience; though I continued to lend my implements on request. Thus they could really learn nothing from me, in the sense of adopting what I thought was proper; but I was educated by them to their ways, over the long run, because of their great patience with me and because I could help them.

I think you are beginning to see that the education of Jules Henry was slow, partly because of my ignorance, partly because of my inflexibility, partly because of necessity and partly because of fear.

Meanwhile it is important to bear in mind that it was up to me to adapt to the Kaingáng, not the other way around, for I was a stranger among them, presuming on their hospitality and on their sense of responsibility for me – they never let me out of their sight in the jungle for fear I would get lost or hurt.

It was much easier for me to accept the Kaingáng attitude towards sex than towards property because I was less hard-nosed about sex than about private property. It is a striking feature of our culture that, although it is more relaxed about sex than fifty years ago, our pristine selfishness is still with us; and generosity can be exercised on a broad scale only when we think it will do us some good – like foreign aid. At any rate, in the course of his life every adult male Kaingáng has sex with almost every adult female.[1] Since the groups are small this is not difficult. But in and out of marriage this goes on. The most striking features of this activity are that there is practically no jealousy even in extra-marital affairs and that men and women never lose a sense of responsibility for each other and for each other's children. Among these primitive 'redskins' there is no sexuality without responsibility, and this is really at the heart of their widespread sexual activity, for they build their sense of responsibility around sexuality and are the most responsible people in the world. Thus, in a startling way, what looks to us like promiscuity turns out to be a kind of strict ethical system. This is another example of cross-cultural education – the education of Jules Henry to the view that not all ethical systems are built on Judeo-Christian principles.

I think you will not have failed to notice that I have been very critical of myself, of my stupidity during my first field trip – indeed my first trip outside the United States. If I had been more aware of myself, more able to perceive the far-reaching consequences of my own automatic reactions, I would have been a better field worker; or in other words, have better educated myself. Thus cross-cultural education requires self-knowledge.

I will now deal one by one with the experiences of which I have spoken. First is the matter of the unsolicited kindness. In this situation I was in the position of learning from the Kaingáng; or, to put it in the jargon of sociology, I, a member of the dominant culture, was in a position to learn from the subordinate culture, but I was unable to do so for a long time because I was too bound to my own ways. As teachers we find it difficult to *learn* from those we are supposed to *teach* because to learn from them would be to reverse our roles, and that is generally humiliating. Learning from the *taught* is an ideal of our culture, yet we think it so extraordinary when we do that a teacher who says of his pupils, 'They taught me a lot' is supposed to be

1. Sexual relations exclude 'only parents and blood siblings'. Jules Henry, *Jungle People* (New York, 1964), p. 33.

admired because he has done an unusual thing. I suggest that learning from those we teach should be as routine as putting one foot in front of another while walking. Every move a child makes, every word he utters, every expression on his face gives occasion for learning from him.

In the matter of unsolicited kindness, then, I was a learner because I am a member of a culture in which kindness unsolicited is a surprise: it occurs, but not routinely. Among the Kaingáng it is routine, and what they did for one another was not deemed kindness. What is most striking in all this is that we can, without knowing it, be violating a people's very existence. In this case the Kaingáng were *not* insulted when I paid them, but often, we can, and we do, without knowing it, violate a people's sense of existence – even when we think we are kind. Hence those people, those 'others' whose existence we violate, may appear surprised or shocked or even ungrateful when we do what we consider the 'right thing'.

To continue with the discussion of payment for kindness: I was unaware the Indians were learning anything about me; yet they were always studying me, and, I might add, putting up with me. Thus those we try to learn about are always learning about us, just as our educational *subjects* are always sizing us up. They size us up and they learn to put up with us. Putting up with a member of a strange culture is a strain: we think the Mexicans or the Negroes or the poor are a strain: think of what a strain we are to them!

The Kaingáng learnt from me that they would be rewarded for services; but then their desire for what I had got the better of them, and I had decided to accept no more favours; they had to find a way to get what they dearly wanted. So they demanded it. Thus under the driving stimulus of incalculable treasure, they confronted an American in a most complicated way. Let me be clear: I had stimulated them by rewarding little favours; I had awakened expectations, and then cut them off. Meanwhile there I was, a veritable storehouse of treasure. How to get it? They could not imagine what to do. I had rejected their services. They were strongly desiring and they were intoxicated. The thing to do was to demand. Yet they were confronting a person with ideas entirely different from theirs.

Thus a number of things had happened: 1. I had awakened hopes and dashed them. 2. I had much to give and would not yield it. 3. I had a great big ego problem. 4. The Kaingáng did not know how to reach their desire in terms that I would understand; they could only express their desire in terms they understood, to wit, that nobody has the right to hold on to property that others want. Then as we talked and talked under the deepening twilight an idea suddenly occurred to them – not to me – that solved *our* difficult problem. They emerged more intelligent than I, for *they* solved the problem not I; the 'inferior' beings, as they are often imagined to be, had the answer, not the trained brain. And their solution, even exchange, was precisely in terms of my own culture. From this we can draw the moral that it is not always the so-called superior being who can solve his own problems even in his own terms. Also, let us observe, that the Kaingáng did not want a fight. I still remember how they stood with their guns and lances in their hands, yet made no effort to intimidate me with them; they merely sounded aroused. Thus they were not trying to scare me. Thus, and this seems to me so tremendously important in all confrontations between learner and teacher, *there was no ego point at issue at all*. Perceive how simple the issue was for them and how enormously complicated it was for me. Hence another message: when strangers meet it is a good guess that what is in A's head is not in B's.

Perceive now that the Indians deemed themselves poor, placed small value on what they had and had no experience of bargaining. Thus they misperceived themselves and this misperception went hand in hand with lack of experience. What did they know about wheeling and dealing? Thus between us the abyss was created by their underestimation of themselves and by the lack of experience of both of us. What it amounted to was ignorance of each other's culture. It is essential in all situations of cross-cultural education that both parties estimate themselves and each other adequately and that each search out the areas of inexperience in the other. Underestimation and lack of experience in dealing with particular situations are prime causes of communications breakdown.

But it is essential that there be no fear, that there be good will on both sides and that each be given plenty of time to come to a decision. Neither the Kaingáng nor I had anything against the other; they were not afraid of me and I was not frightened enough of the non-existent threat to do the wrong thing. Meanwhile, as I talked without cease, I gave them the chance to solve the problem I was unable to solve myself. But meanwhile, also, they were patient. From this we derive the conclusion that when A drags things out it may be because he can find no solution to a problem that seems very simple to B, who must therefore not lose patience but try to solve their mutual problem himself.

I was wrong in my assumption that they were trying to intimidate me – or even that they would infer from this one instance my general vulnerability to a display of determination. It is clear now that my youthful ego played some part in bringing about the decision we made that evening many years ago in the jungle beside the river and that I misunderstood the ego situation. Let me give another example from my experience with the Kaingáng. Before I went into the forest with them on the first long hunt, I trained hard, for I knew life would be difficult. I swam back and forth across the narrow river many times each day and I did callisthenics. By the time I entered the jungle I was in pretty good shape, so that the long marches up and down the mountains and the pursuit of wild animals did not fatigue me. When, however, we came back to the post and I started to work with informants, sitting and writing day after day, I grew soft. One day as I was working with a Kaingáng informant the cry of 'Jacutinga' – a large game-bird – went up around the village and I grabbed my shotgun and took off with the Indians headed up the mountainside to hunt the birds. Of course, it was too much for me, and I had to lie down beside the trail. I do not recall for how many weeks I felt sheepish for having caved in, and I constantly looked for sly grins and pointed remarks from the Indians, but there were none. In almost any remark they made I was prepared to hear an allusion to my weakness. Yet, as I came to know their folklore, as I listened to their conversation for many months, I heard no reference to that kind of weakness. The weakness that was outstanding in their folklore was desertion – desertion of another Kaingáng attacked by the enemy; weakness in the man who spent too much time chasing women. As for my brand of masculinity, perseverence in the face of overwhelming fatigue, and success with women, such values never occurred in folklore or conversation at all. Thus my kind of masculine ego was no part of their culture. The point is that over and over and over again we find sympathy for weakness, not contempt, and a total unawareness of some of our most dearly held values. The point is that across cultures egos rarely match; the point is that what might seem mere natural ego defence to us becomes meaningless to others. In my experience with other cultures I have found sympathy for or unawareness of factors that seem so essential to the ego in my own culture. I would say that on the whole in communicating across cultures the ego is best left in the tent, while one deals with the reality outside.

Much has been said about differences in values. Present preoccupation with values in education is something like trying to put a new face on somebody who has seen better days, for beneath the study of values lies the same old monster, education. Under the mask lie the same rigid convictions and the same emphasis on our own values: when middle-class teachers teach about Zulus or Mexicans the children cannot be reached because the rest of the time they are taught implicitly or explicitly, by books or by the attitudes of the teachers, that there is one value system that sets the limits of our own pre-Columbian value out-look and that is our own.

Fundamentally we cannot teach other people's values. What we can do is, perhaps, make children less fearful about our own: make it possible for them to speculate about their validity and whether adults really live up to them, make it possible for them to think without fear about other possibilities, make it possible for them to hold their values but without such intense ego involvement that they will be like the anthropologist panting with fatigue beneath a jungle tree and frightened that the Indians will think him chicken. I have heard of 'tolerance of other people's values', let me suggest the possibility of viewing our own values without fear.

What is Education?

Before going further it is necessary to spend some time on a shapeless topic: what is education? What education is can best be understood, I think, by comparing what middle-class children *learn* from formal curricula and what they *become*. Whatever they learn of reading, writing, arithmetic, pot-holder making, flower-pasting and so on, merely gives them the opportunity to express what they are and what they will become – highly competitive, achieving, ambitious, spendthrift Americans, oriented towards a high standard of living, loving only their nearest and dearest, and for the rest of the time feeling emotionally isolated and terrified of strange social ideas. These personality traits, these learnt character traits, are of flesh and blood, incorporated like food into the bone, flesh and blood: the children's American value orientations, which are part of them, is what has really been learnt. They may never use what they learnt at the desk, and so forget it; never make a pot-holder again, read nothing but menus after they have got out of school. But they cannot divest themselves of their American character – it will accompany them to the grave. Education consists then in making what is available for learning part of one's self, so that one cannot think without it, and never forget it. Cross-cultural education, therefore, would be a kind of education in which one automatically thought not in terms of the conditions of the other culture but in terms of mankind. I cannot identify with a real Mexican, Negro, Egyptian or Vietnamese, because they are all so different; but I can try to be a human being. I am afraid that the more I learn to specify the differences between me and all those 'others', the more I feel separate from them. While it is true that the differences are real and that understanding is necessary, the sharing of a common humanity is primary. I would say then that education is becoming a certain kind of person as well as absorbing certain textual materials; but that in cross-cultural education the former is fundamental.

Cross-Cultural Education and the Self

I turn now to even more trying problems of cross-cultural education. A teacher is always talking about himself as well as about the subject matter. As he stands before the class he is saying, whether he is aware of it or not, 'This is I'; and surely his students, whether they or the teacher are aware of it or not, are always learning about the teacher through his manner of communicating the subject. It is true that in elementary and high school, what the teacher teaches is often so stereotyped by the books used that it would seem impossible for him to say anything about himself in, let us say, arithmetic, yet he obviously is, by the way he presents the material and how he manages the class. Always, as he teaches, therefore, the teacher is saying something about what he believes and always presenting a certain image of himself. The implicit communication of a belief and the implicit presentation of a self-image become particularly relevant when communicating across cultures, for then the possibility that we attempt to communicate one thing or present ourselves in one light while actually being different, threatens the very possibility of communication. To present ourselves as tolerant while being basically discriminating, to talk as if we were honest when we are not, to attempt to urge cooperation while fostering competition undermines our relationship to those we attempt to teach.

Thus cross-cultural education is possible only when the teacher realizes that he does not live up to his own values and that therefore to attempt to teach them as if he did is sham. Cross-cultural education becomes a possibility only when the educator has looked within himself and asked 'Who am I and what do I stand for?' and 'What is *my* culture really, and what does *it* stand for?' It becomes a possibility only when one realizes that, although few of one's friends live up to their spoken values, the matter is never discussed. The reason for this is fear, for the inward fear counsels us not to look at ourselves privately, and the outer one tells us never to do it in public, and never to compel our friends to do it either.

The Great Issues of Mankind

... I saw that kindness consisted in saying, 'You are welcome, at the dinner table'; that piety consisted in going to communion once a year. This I saw, and I laughed.[2]

Throughout history, everywhere as an inescapable aspect of becoming human, mankind has confronted certain great issues. Whether in the fields and cities of Europe or Asia, whether among the tribes and villages of Africa, in the jungles of South America, on the islands and atolls of the Pacific or on the ice floes of the Arctic, mankind has confronted these issues of which I shall speak, although they have presented themselves to him differently depending on the conditions of his life.

First there is religion. Everywhere the supernatural has been formulated by man in a different way. The Judeo-Christian tradition has developed the idea of God and of a Holy Trinity,

2. From S. Kierkegaard, *Either/Or*, New York, 1959, p. 33.

and central to the religious conceptions of the Jews and the Christians are the ideas of love and creative power. Like a parent, God years for His children to love Him as He loves them, and the Old Testament idea of the jealous God has been superseded by the longing One in whom love predominates. Central to the Judeo-Christian system are its ethical ideas, so that honesty, truth, non-violence, love of parents and so on are anchored in our supernatural system, and godliness has become inseparable from human decency. From this it follows that all who are treated indecently would necessarily be sceptical of the Judeo-Christian system and quite unwilling to accept their misery as punishment for their sins.

One of the most interesting anthropological findings is that in most of the world there is no connection between ethics and religion. While in the more refined dimensions of Hinduism – known to possibly one or two per cent of India's hundreds of millions – there is a relationship between ethics and religion, most of the peasants and the workers in the cities derive their ethical attitudes from social relations. Confucianism and primitive Buddhism established no specific connection between violating ethical principles and offending God. Almost without exception this is true of tribal cultures also. The effort to establish the goodness of any principle on the basis of religion, therefore, must cope with the fact that ours is an almost unique formulation. It must cope with the fact that for most people ethics, even in our own society, is based on the social situation, and that the people who constantly think about the relation of ethics to God are a handful.

Another issue that arises in the context of religion is what we like to call tolerance, which means that, although we do not follow the other person's form of religion, would not permit our child to marry him, would not dream of setting foot inside his house of worship, we recognize his right to his religion. The point is that we do not consider him strange and that on the whole we like to believe that we do not consider him subversive of eternal principles. Yet many people do, even in our own country, and cross-cultural education has always to cope with those who are willing to give lip service to tolerance but practise intolerance.

Thus the separation of religion and ethics in most of the world outside our borders and our acceptance of tolerance in word and its violation in deed are two obstacles to the handling of religion in cross-cultural communication. Another obstacle is that we are merely Sabbath Jews and Christians.

Possibly more important than religion among the great issues of mankind is that of freedom, slavery and privilege. We have a folklore of freedom, slavery and privilege, which exalts heroes who have fought and sometimes died for what we call freedom, who have fought against slavery and privilege. Yet it is not at all necessary that everyone accept that folklore, and surely many must be repelled by it – especially those who, even in the midst of people who accept the folklore of freedom, are yet punished by them. If I were lecturing on freedom and some child with a dark face were to rise up and say, 'I spit upon your freedom', he would be right. If some winter day I were lecturing on the reduction of privilege in our society and some child in a thin coat were to cry out, 'I am shivering in the cold of your democracy', he would be right. And if some child whose father chops cotton or picks lettuce at the minimum wage were to shout from his seat, 'Who says there is no more slavery?' I would have to say that he is right.

Thus if we put together those among us who are not free and those who are underprivileged, there are millions to whom our message about the great issues of mankind would seem absurd, hypocritical and even evil. I hope you are beginning to understand that our own formulations, our own reading, our own folklore about the great issues of mankind are not at once translatable into the language of different cultures.

Another great issue, found more among the high civilizations of Europe, America and the Far East than in tribal societies, though it is by no means missing there, is that of riches and luxury versus poverty. Most elementary-school textbooks avoid this issue by locating all scenes in farms and suburbs and by dressing the picture children in the latest styles. We do not know specifically what the reaction of poor city children is to such distortion, but the point is that beginning with elementary school and on into high school a great issue of the great cultures is begged. The fact that since what are called great civilizations have been achieved only at the cost of a bitter contrast between luxury and squalor, there is some question as to this greatness. The fact that the greatness is emphasized and the squalor hidden robs children of an intellectual and emotional experience, and surely must have the result of making poor children merely apathetic, and of gradually making a teacher's position untenable in social studies.

In teaching about the great issues of mankind one's own smallness is apt to become apparent to the eyes of children. I hope you understand that I am not merely saying that bad textbooks do not teach children. I *am* saying that the great issues of mankind cannot be taught if we are not frank, if we do not know ourselves, if we are afraid to confront the fact that we do not observe our own values. Of course, if one does not think that the great issues of mankind should ever be presented, there is no argument. But then neither can one talk about the Pilgrims, the Revolutionary War, the Civil War and so on.

A fourth great issue of mankind is that of violence versus non-violence, war versus peace. When we talk about our wars we imply always that justice has been on our side and that war is an eternal way of settling disputes. What I wish to emphasize is the fact that the teacher, in teaching about war, often unwittingly reinforces in the mind of his students the view that in the United States violence is as natural as breathing. Or, in cross-cultural terms, she communicates the naturalness of the idea of war to all the strangers before her. There is really not much difference between the way our wars are taught in school and the way *Have Gun will Travel*, *Laramie* or *The Man from Uncle* are presented on television; for in all of them killing is taken for granted; and children can get the idea that problems are best solved by slaughtering the opposition. There is no point to teaching about wars unless the idea is communicated that, given the present state of human cupidity, entanglement and ignorance, no other way to solve problems has been found. In all TV the defeat of evil is the consequence of superior craft and power and what becomes clear is that right is on the side of the cleverest, the most powerful, and the fastest gun. The inference is then clear, and any child, and any deprived ethnic, could make it, viz. that if you are clever, powerful and fast you will be right. Other messages equally clear are that the people who are always right are those on my side, that we are always better looking than the enemy, and that people in the right do not usually talk with a foreign accent. Though Batman is a moron he is better looking than his enemies, so we can tell he is on the side of justice, even though he is stupid. The most intriguing innovation in *Have Gun will Travel* is that the hero is so ugly he looks like a bad guy.

However we may pay lip service to gentleness, our history is a violent one; and the Watts riots express the ancient and unresolved dichotomies between freedom and slavery, luxury and poverty, and violence and non-violence. They are an expression of the bankruptcy of values, the evil of society and of the falseness of the idea of cross-cultural education in the presence of cynical injustice. Perhaps I am trying to say that where justice, or at least compassion, prevails cross-cultural education is unnecessary and that there is some danger that the latter take the place of the former because the former is impossible for us. I am saying that compassion can take the place of cross-cultural education, but that, being what we are, we have to accept the latter.

The struggle of knowledge to assert itself over ignorance is another great issue. History recounts that gifted men and women have been reviled, tortured and killed by the ignorant; and that men often hate those who present strange ideas. Nowadays we no longer torment, imprison or excommunicate those with revolutionary ideas in science. The person who is in danger is the one who has revolutionary ideas about society. In tribal societies maturity consists in part in understanding that what one knows is all there is to know, all that is worth while knowing; and it is interesting to examine that state of mind in connection with our own. In regard to science we are taught that there is much more to know than what we already know and that any moment what we know may turn out to be obsolete because of a new discovery. In everything else matters are very different, however, especially in social ideas. Today we are convinced that our social forms are best; tomorrow it must be the same. On the other hand, when we look at other societies different from ours, we still know that ours is best and that those others ought to be transformed to be like ours. Let us, we say, give them our compassion and hope they will evolve without the first cavalry. Why this strange division, to think that our own society must be as it is but that all different from it must change? Why do we take unchanging social sameness for granted in ourselves and change in the direction of ourselves, with respect to others? It is this assumption of constancy over here and change over there which, when challenged, is most likely to stimulate persecution. It is this assumption of constancy that offers major road-blocks in cross-cultural education.

I knew an anthropologist interested in the kibbutzim, those socialistically oriented agricultural communities in Israel which for a long time were a wall defending Israel against outside enemies. In speaking of the reasons the kibbutznics gave for remaining there, he said that, as explanation, they simply parroted kibbutz socialistic ideologies and anti-capitalist propaganda. How could he learn from them, if he believed they were merely parroting? But the kibbutznics are human beings. So between the student and them cross-cultural education was well-nigh impossible because he came from a different social system and, however he gave lip-service to tolerance of the social ideologies of others, he rejected them; in his heart he knew they were wrong. And in his heart he knew they were wrong because he had learnt to be an American better than he had learnt to be an anthropologist. What he and the kibbutznics would learn from one another was that each was incapable of the inner experience of the other; that they could both talk Hebrew but that they were shouting at each other across an abyss of uninvolvement. Thus one might say that, although they knew each other's point of view, they were ignorant of it.

The next great issue to be discussed is that of selfishness versus solicitude. Throughout our history in stories, drama and in history these have been contrasted with one another, and the struggle between them goes on in each of us. The concept of gratitude itself derives from our preoccupation with selfishness, to the degree that we have this special word – gratitude – to label any action that seems beyond the call of duty.

The question is where does this conflict leave the teacher? Ordinarily the teacher believes she has paid her respects to the problem by telling the children to help one another; and she feels deeply gratified if David helps Archie with his arithmetic. It turns out to be especially gratifying if Archie is an 'ethnic', for in that case the ideals have been served. Archie's problem, however, is that he lives in a selfish world where people have to be induced to give and that they give in expectation of return. When David is not under the eye of the teacher, furthermore, he may be just as self-centred as anybody else. When the inducement of the teacher's favour is missing, where there is no expectation of return, David may not be interested in being kind.

The problem that we face here, whether we are dealing with cross-cultural education or education without trimmings, is that the incidental message communicated to Archie has little to do with his everyday experience of discrimination. Shall the teacher therefore not encourage David? Of course not; it is always better to have a cooperative classroom. But the central problem is that this great issue of mankind, as between selfishness and solicitude, is not going to be resolved in favour of the latter when the culture is oriented towards selfishness; when the culture in which Archie lives daily impresses him with the coldness of the haves.

In our culture a child's entire training pushes him away from the universal components of ethical goodness, so that selfishness becomes part of his body. Let us try to imagine David at two years. If he tries to give a toy away his mother will point out to him that it is his, that Grandpa gave it to him and that Grandpa would be unhappy to discover David didn't have it any more – that he thought so little of Grandpa that he gave the toy away. Furthermore it probably cost Grandpa a lot of money. In this way David's natural impulses to generosity begin to dry up. As David staggers about the house he is attracted by objects he sees in the various rooms of his middle-class house: his mother's manicure set, his father's socks, his sister's artificial braids – fascinating objects all of them. But they are not his. This is another way in which he learns about possessiveness, about private property, about holding on to what is yours. Such learnings merely fit him for the larger society.

Similar considerations apply to love, and we know that love is part of generosity. We all know David: he is friendly, he likes to sit on almost anybody's lap, even to putting his arms around the neck of random adults who smell right, smile right and are cuddly enough. But there has to be a limit to this, for if it goes too far it makes his mother anxious to see David love too many other people: his *family* is where his love belongs, and mother quietly explains to David that *she* is his mummy and not Mrs Bellows or Mrs Thomas. So David learns to keep his love and his possessions at home and to himself.

Since from his earliest days David has been taught to be

selfish and to contain his love, he cannot usually do much for Archie outside the classroom; and since Archie lives in a selfish world he is not going to believe, from the classroom, that the world outside is just like it.

I have not completed the list of great issues of mankind. There are others: the struggle of integrity versus exploitation, the issue of individuality versus the collectivity, the problem of the state versus the individual. These are all major threads that run through the history of mankind, and which appear in one form or another in the course of going to school and being a teacher. Yet there is no time to talk about them here. What I have tried to do is to present some of the great issues, to suggest how they confront us in education and to speculate about what direction examination of the problems might take in cross-cultural education.

Conclusions

Beginning with my wanderings in the forests of Brazil I have taken you on a rambling course through the jungle dimness of an educational idea: cross-cultural education. It is a powerful one, but, like all powerful humanistic ideas, it requires a profound change in personality in order that it may become part of life and practice. Cross-cultural education requires that teacher and learner become something different. Really that they become human beings instead of Americans, Russians, Frenchmen, Negroes, etc. – an amazing improbability! Still there *are* such deep yearnings in many of us, and the more war darkens our lives with the blood-stained question 'What does it mean to be *merely* American?' the greater the possibility that we may see that the most rewarding experience is to be human.

12. Ecumenism: An Anthropological View*

. . . sin must properly have its ground . . . in the activity with which a man has laboured to obscure his intelligence.

Søren Kierkegaard[1]

You have asked me to talk about ecumenism from the anthropological point of view. Anthropology, with its view of man from the origin of the species, through his incredible and startling originality of development in culture and physical type over the land masses and islands of the world, cannot think of ecumenism as conceived by Christianity only; for while Christianity is concerned with a special religious development unique in history and confined to a minority of the world population, it cannot by itself be the concern of anthropology, which has pretences to universality through time and place. Anthropology, properly conceived, cannot but think of the unity of *mankind* rather than of the unity within a particular religion, which has, almost since its inception, been riven by quarrels in which all participants felt so threatened it was often difficult for them to separate matters of faith from feelings of personal or even political vulnerability. Much of this is in the past, but many of the problems are still with us.

Anthropology, in considering the unity of mankind, holds within the mind's eye the slant-eyed peoples of Mongolia, China Paleo-Siberia and all of the Indians of America, even long before the coming of the white man. The Eskimos, the Yellow

* Parts of this essay have been previously published in two earlier works: 'Is education possible? Are we qualified to enlighten dissenters?' Donald A. Erikson (Ed.) *Public Controls in Nonpublic Schools*, University of Chicago, 1969: Murray L. Wax, Stanley Diamond and Fred O. Gearing (Eds.) *Anthropological Prospectives in Education*, Basic Books, New York 1971.

1. *Fear and Trembling* and *The Sickness Unto Death*, Oxford, 1969, p. 229.

Knives and the Dog Rib of the Yukon Valley; the Ojibways of the woodlands of Canada and of the north central States, the unspeakably cruel Indians of Nova Scotia and the north-eastern United States, who formerly tortured; the Aztecs and Mayas of Mexico, the Quechua-speaking peoples of the South American highlands and the agricultural Indians of the Amazon and Orinoco – and so on down to the Indians of Tierra del Fuego, whose ethnography has been beautifully executed by Catholic priests. And so to Africa, among the tribes of highland, desert and coast who are now erupting into new freedoms, new disasters and new cruelties. He perceives the suffering slant-eyed peoples of Vietnam, akin in language to the Chinese, dying under the rain of our bombs and artillery, while they defend themselves. He looks last, perhaps, at the modern European peoples and at diversities at home – whites, Negroes, Jews, Christians, Italians, Old Americans, Poles and so on – and he thinks then of *the unity of mankind*. Besides this immensity of the unity of the species, all other issues of unity pale. For anthropology *does* conceive mankind to be a single species, *homo sapiens*, endowed everywhere with the same capacities for logical thought, for love, for hate, for creativity and religious experience. What he sees is that the way thought, love, hate, creativity and religious experiences develop is different in different places; but he discerns now that even such differences are insignificant when compared with the universal striving towards social betterment. It is a striking discovery for me that the Zulus, the Chinese, the Vietnamese, the Ashanti, the peoples of the Cameroons, the Mariannas and the Aleuts – wherever you find the human species regardless of colour, language or religious beliefs – want a better life; and man will fight for it and wet the ground with blood if he does not get it. I say, compared to the unity of mankind in mind and capabilities, compared to the unity of mankind in striving for a better physical existence, all other unities seem secondary. I speak for myself, but out of an anthropological background.

Today the whole world is exploding in one single cry, though those who utter it may not know they utter it. This cry is, 'We shall not be starved and degraded!' Let there be no doubt about this: from the unspeakable *favelas*, the hillside slums of Rio de Janeiro, to the cane fields of Salta, to the slums of the American ghettos, the rice paddies of South-East Asia and the huts and kraals of Africa, the cry is one. This is the unity that strikes me. It is this unity with which *we* all have to deal; it is this unity which we must accomplish or join one another in the unity of the grave, never having completed the task assigned us – to become human and humane to one another. If churchmen quibble about their denominational prerogatives it can be only because they have nothing better to think about; only because they do not understand the real unity that miraculously awaits them – the unity of the human race. The problem of Christianity now is not ecumenism within itself, but the simple, humble ecumenism of humanity. I say therefore to members of all denominations and religions, whether Christian, Jewish, Mohammedan, Buddhist or Hindu, it is time to join the human race.

Let us now turn to some of the issues that divide mankind and make all men vulnerable and separate them from one another. I deal first with the issue of political economy. Political economy is a term fallen into disuse since the nineteenth century, but it may well be restored to the vocabulary of the social sciences, for it is the discipline that deals with economics and politics as one single branch of thought. Political economy is the discipline that points out that a system of economic corporate enterprise is inseparable from our kind of political system, while the Soviet system of state ownership of all but a few small agricultural activities is inseparable from a communist form of political organization.

Since 1917 almost a third of the earth's surface and a third of its people have developed political economies radically different from our own. These are the peoples who have already become socialist, while other millions want it. Mrs Gandhi, Prime Minister of India and friend of the United States, has been constantly under attack at home for seeming to abandon India's socialist ideals. The emergence of a new socialist humanity has been accompanied by the disappearance or extreme weakening of many capitalist powers, to the degree that, feeling beleaguered amidst the diminishing strength of its allies, America has devoted an ever larger proportion of its gross national product to its military establishment.

The rise of socialism and the doubling of the number of violent revolutions since 1958 has left the United States with such an extreme feeling of vulnerability that one wonders whether it can tolerate enlightenment, for enlightenment always involves a re-examination of basic assumptions about political economy.

Since 1939 the central position of armaments in the American economy, the fact that the arms industries are its 'balance wheel', as one presidential commission put it, the fact that the *balance wheel* has become the *pivotal gear*, growing in importance each decade with our fear, is now taken for granted, because the fear has become domesticated. We are like those Africans among whom schistosomiasis is endemic, so that they think bloody urine is normal; or like the Kaingáng Indians whose teeth are so rotten that they wondered whether mine were real.

When we ask therefore, under what conditions is enlightenment possible, and realize that it seems possible only when fears are few, while our own are numerous, we must wonder about our own possibilities.

With such general considerations in view, I shall examine the problem under the following headings: Political Economy, the Gross National Product, War, the Historic Necessity of Stupidity, the Occupational System, Leisure, Vulnerability, and Narrowness.

Political Economy. The citizens of any society must be taught to believe that their form of political economy is the only satisfactory existence. In our own society this is accomplished not only through verbal depreciation of other types of political economy but, especially in the lower grades of school, by presenting educational materials as if decent human existence occurred in our type of political economy only. Elementary arithmetic, even the new mathematics, is presented in narrow middle-class settings. All of this restricts the possibilities of enlightenment.

Gross National Product. At no point may anything be taught that might interfere with the gross national product. This means not only that materials suggesting the possibility of an austere life, or one dedicated to *materially unproductive* activity, must be excluded from, or muted in curricula, but also that people must be portrayed as spenders. Clothes designers must surely have been employed to develop illustrations for current elementary-school readers, for when the *Dick and Jane* series tells about the activities of the same family in a succession of stories, the entire family is wearing a different and attractive set of clothes in each story.

It is now necessary to explain the reasons for a phenomenon that frightens most Americans – revolutions from the left; for it is as certain as the ocean and the sky that, regardless of armed force or the intervention of religion, we shall live with these revolutions from the left for a long time to come; so that it is our duty to understand them, rather than to react like infants, with blind rage, to what irritates us, and to continue the division of mankind into armed camps.

A revolution from the left is loosely defined by the world as one which tries to make property change hands: the taking from those 'who have' by those who 'have not'. When my wife and I were in Argentina years ago studying the Indians of the Gran Chaco, we went on a little vacation for a while, as a relief from the frightful heat, to lovely Raco, a spot in the foothills of the Andes. One day, on a horseback ride, I was taken to the top of a low mountain that commanded an immense view of the surrounding country. I was told that as far as I could see in any direction the land belonged to Patron —.[2] Some months later when the Indians went to work on the sugar-cane plantations of Patron —,[3] some distance from this spot, my wife and I went with them. The Indians were living on a narrow strip of ground, where they had thrown up shelters made of dried-up old sugar cane. Their water supply was the irrigation canals that fed the cane, and the garbage of the mill was dumped among the canals. My wife and I lived in a tent in the middle of the Indian camp. All the *loteros*, that is, the men in charge of each section of cane, were armed but the Indians were not, and the town was owned by the mill. Patron — himself and more than one *lotero* were state senators. The police station of the town was an armoury: the town was the mill and the chief of police was an employee. While we were there some Indians of a different tribe, far away on another section, wanted to go home before the administration wished and they were shot. All of this, except the shooting, my wife and I saw with our own eyes.

I tell you this in order that you may begin to understand the nature of revolutions from the left and why they have the character they do. In underdeveloped countries *not having* means a life of continued unspeakable poverty and filth with no hope of change because, since the haves *are* the government, they are beyond the influence of the poor. It is also necessary to understand that *having* means having the country in a real, concrete, material, palpable, countable sense. I am sure that you can readily understand the difficulties in changing such a situation by peaceful means. The problem is that throughout the underdeveloped countries the problem has mainly this shape and that it is agrarian. Most of the land is held by big landlords, and small holdings are difficult to maintain because they yield so little, and sudden expenses undercut income, which leads to

2. Name withheld.
3. Same man.

mortgaging, which leads eventually to loss. Often the larger holdings are not as big as that of Patron — but, relative to the total available land, they are big enough. In these countries, also, the land is constantly subdivided by inheritance, so that plots get smaller and smaller. The circular process is indeed vicious: the piece of land becomes so small that it is not enough to support a family, so the man or the family goes out to work; but since they cannot then give adequate attention to their little piece of land the yield is so small that what labour is put into it is not economic, the patch goes to weeds and is at last sold for a song.

One of the things that few understand is the enormous expenses peasants have in underdeveloped countries. Outstanding, perhaps, is the expense of disease, for since they are always getting sick they have to hire medicine men and these are often costly. A series of illnesses may impoverish a family, force them to mortgage their property and turn them into *peons* or force them off the land altogether. Almost any important event in the life of such a peasant may cost him a great deal of money, from births, through marriage, disease and death. Funerals may be exceedingly expensive and so force the survivors into debt. It is impossible in a short speech to inform you of all the factors that contribute to misery and ultimately to revolution from the left in underdeveloped countries. But I shall mention two more that are critically important: since peasant holdings tend to be small – I have seen some about six feet square in Ixmiquilpan in Mexico – it is impossible to use modern machinery; and since the peasants are poor and the land exhausted, necessary fertilizers cannot be bought. This whole process of marginal living facilitates the loss of the tiny holding to the man who has much.

Finally I must remind you that the physical suffering entailed is accompanied by a humiliation as of the dirt. When, then, we put together the physical degradation with the spiritual one, we can readily understand why revolutions from the left may be characterized by unheard-of ferocities – or, at least, let us say, ferocities paralleled by those of the war in Vietnam.

When such a revolution from the left succeeds it remains for years in a state of disequilibrium, not only because of general problems of readjustment, but because those who had the land taken away from them, those whose new holdings are now only about the same size as those of all the other peasants, or perhaps a little larger, never give up trying to get the land back. The result can be a holocaust such as we saw recently in Indonesia where, communist power having been undermined, thousands of peasants (called 'communists' by our press) who had got new lands were killed by former landlords. An underdeveloped country wishing to liquidate its landlord problem has several choices: 1. Simple expropriation and redistribution without compensation but with equal division for everybody. 2. Expropriation with payment. 3. Expropriation with larger holdings being given to the expropriated class. In expropriation pure and simple the danger of ferocious counter-revolution is grave. That is why revolutionaries sometimes kill so many landlords. In expropriation with larger holdings sometimes given to the former landlords, as in Egypt, you have perhaps the most stable possibility. But expropriation with payment provides one of the most serious dilemmas for an underdeveloped country – like India, for example, where a just payment for the land by the new government impoverishes the national treasury, prevents development and fosters poverty and revolution.

When I went to Brazil thirty years ago I was stunned, for although I had seen the people in the slums of New York, I had never been in a place where thousands of people walked the streets in patchwork clothing. You have seen patchwork quilts – they are made by sewing hundreds of little pieces of cloth together; this was the clothing of thousands that I saw in Brazil – but they were clean.

I think you may now be able to understand the revolutions from the so-called left. Often they have nothing to do with communism and have no ideology but the wish for land and a decent existence. That members of the extreme left should become attached to them is no more surprising than that the Birchers and Minutemen should get attached to the Republican party; yet no one in his right mind thinks of the Republican party as exclusively John Birch.

I must go on with this analysis of revolution from the left because it is the principle factor dividing mankind at the present time and the understanding of it and the right reaction to it will determine whether we survive or not.

One of the astounding achievements of the United States is the ability to restrain profits while paying a reasonable wage to workers. Some may gasp at this assertion in the light of labour's complaint that they are not receiving their just share of the immense profits realized by American industry in the 1960s. However right they may be, and I think they are, the profits of American industry are small compared to the return on investment in underdeveloped countries. The reason for this is that no businessman in an underdeveloped country, as anybody can see who reads the papers, can be sure from day to day whether he will be in business tomorrow, whether he will be in gaol, bankrupt, taxed beyond measure or rich beyond dreams. The result is that in order to be induced to go into business at all he must make spectacular profits, with the result that his workers get low wages, and the seeds of revolution are sown again. If we ask then why American democracy cannot be exported, the answer must be that such export is the dream of an ignorant person, because the conditions for export are simply not present in other countries. What is present, rather, are the conditions for revolutions from the left; which means, on the whole, the rising up of poor people who cannot stand the suffering and the humiliation any longer.

I return now to some initial remarks. I said that we have been taught to think of our own form of political economy as the only one fit for mankind and that such a conception separates us from others of a different persuasion and need; and I said that our own feeling of vulnerability in the presence of the surge towards socialism prevents us from thinking clearly and from joining the rest of the human race. I hope I have given some insight into the factors involved and the effort that must be made to overcome our fear. I turn now to the problem of war.

War. School does not interfere with the idea that all wars fought by the United States are just. Nothing must be presented there that suggests that we could have done anything to avoid them, or that war is an unthinkable solution to contemporary problems. Pious sighs over the horrors of war have always been permitted, and sundry generals quoted, but little insight is given into war's causes, into American responsibility, into the general human responsibility for entertaining the possibility of war, or into the possibility of our citizens having the right to reject the bellicosity of its statesmen. Since the most important thing for a child to learn is that the United States must always have freedom to choose war when it pleases, nothing can be taught to dim this view. We cannot, for example, teach that violence is the last resort of even madmen, that a population has a right to voice its fierce objection to war, or that hostility in the face of the possibility of universal bloodshed is unconscionable.

Education for docility is the first necessity of a civilization oriented towards war and a danger in enlightenment is that it undermines docility and replaces it with courage. One of the many paradoxes of modern warfare is that it exploits docility to train killers.

All wars nowadays are fought because of differences in political economy and because one nation or section of the population feels threatened by the surging economy or by the economic objectives of another. The fact that these confrontations are based more or less on confusion, stupidity, rigidity and nightmare becomes clear when we consider some of the acts of our recent presidents. One of the hopes of the late President John

F. Kennedy and of Premier Khrushchev was to expand trade between the US and the USSR and make peaceful coexistence possible, and President Johnson has continued the move. Recently we made overtures to China of the same general nature. While animosities built up on previous conditions are not easily resolved, it must be clear to all of you by this time that it is our feeling of vulnerability based on poorly understood modern conditions that divide us and even make the Chinese across the sea seem like monsters. When we come to consider this attitude of embargo and fear, we cannot ignore the fact that much of Europe trades with China in a very lively way and accords her diplomatic recognition while we stand bristling and aloof. Nor, above all, dare we overlook the fact that because we still entertain the credibility of war as an outcome in our relationships with China, our present attitude endures. The possibility of war means only one thing – the impossibility of survival. Let me remind you, as Catholics, that in modern times each succeeding war has seen the Church progressively weakened and its catechumens diminished in number. You all remember that the last war saw Judaism almost disappear from Europe. While I cannot read the daily paper without trembling with rage and anxiety, I am still astonished that those who admit the feasibility of war and call for escalation can sleep at night.

The Historic Necessity for Stupidity. Throughout history, whether among the so-called civilized, or so-called primitive, people have had to be taught to be stupid. For to permit the mind to expand to its outermost capabilities results in a challenge to traditional ways. Hence the paradox that while man is intelligent he must also be trained to be stupid, and that a certain amount of intellectual sabotage must be introduced into all educational systems. It is better to have a somewhat stupid population than one trained beyond the capacities of the culture to absorb intelligence. It is clear that teachers with incisive minds, willing to take their students along all possible logical pathways, willing to entertain all intelligent questions, are a danger to any system. Hence all educational systems must train people to be unintelligent within the limits of the culture's ability to survive. That is to say, there seems to be a cutting point where, if a people are too stupid the culture will fall apart, and where the culture will fall apart if they are too intelligent. The cutting point is where the upward curve of intellect meets the downward curve of culturally necessary stupidity.

Current controversies in education revolve not so much around what students should know, and how they should learn, but how stupid we can permit them to be without wrecking the country and the world. In education for stupidity a nice line has to be drawn between teaching the child how to make obvious inferences and letting him make inferences that are too far-reaching for comfort, between training him to see the validity or the truth of a proposition in plane geometry and in teaching him to perceive the fraudulence of a proposition in advertising, political economy, international relations and so on. Teaching a child to think has obvious perils, and for this reason has always been a delusive goal of education in our culture. In our culture nobody can be taught to think, for example, where private enterprise, war or the gross national product might be threatened.

Socialist countries, of course, have *their* forms of socially necessary stupidity. The fruit of stupidity is invulnerability, for when one has been rendered too stupid to penetrate an issue, one can only follow the crowd and the crowd always follows what is popular and what it thinks is safe, even though it often leads to perdition. In any culture stupidity pays off in the social and political areas over the short run. This being the case there can be little inducement to being intelligent because intelligence leads to separation from the crowd and the crowd wants only to be safe from criticism and to have a good time.

This situation confronts the teacher at the college level in the 'stone wall' effect: students who will not discuss, who will not object, who will not examine, and who are likely to become withdrawn and morose if forced to it by a determined teacher. What most of us encounter in the university are rows of moving hands that obediently write down whatever is said, and one need not worry about voicing the most radical opinions because they merely go into the notebook, along with the algae, ions, historic places, dates and names, equations and the dates of the next test.

Some might argue that since in the present stage of evolution man is unable to develop a social system that will not make millions miserable, organized society would be impossible if everybody was smart because they would see through all shams, and social organization is impossible without sham. Others might argue that if the scales were lifted from the eyes of all, the hands of all might be against all, for each would see that the other is a liar. Some might urge that, since man is incapable of constructing a system without massive flaws, it is better for children to be unable to perceive them.

However, I see no evidence that nature has set a certain pace on the clock of evolution, so that our brains will be regulated until such time as, having constructed a utopia, men may look the truth in the eye without murdering their neighbours. This being the case, I see no choice but to seek enlightenment and introduce it into education.

Occupational Systems. The occupational system in any culture has inexorable requirements because jobs must be filled if the culture is to survive, and in our culture the fundamental outlines of the occupational system are congruent with the economic system and with the requirement of the gross national product. The occupational system is a fixed reality, like the sky, and this is true the world over. It follows that our educational system cannot enlighten regarding the possibilities of the soul, but must train children to fit the available jobs and teach students resignation to the occupational categories of the census bureau.

Children must be taught to accept the idea of fixed occupational niches and be so instructed that the freshman's question, 'Philosophy is interesting, but what can you do with it?' will never become absurd. The question 'What am I doing with my life?' is the enemy of the question 'What job can I get?' The occupational system requires that the question 'Is this what I really want to do?' should not rise into consciousness, for it is an iron law of culture that to the degree that education touches on occupation at all it must not permit the question to exist. Culture as a system of thought must exclude dialectical opposites, for when these are permitted to enter consciousness, they shake a culture to its foundations. The dialectic, however, is a magic quern that grinds out its contradictions no matter where it is; so that socialist countries, where the quern presumably came to rest forever, now have to cope with it too.

Leisure. Nowadays, since there is much talk about leisure, it is necessary to say a few words about this tired subject. For the average person, leisure is the time left to him after he has stopped working for pay. That is to say, for the overwhelming bulk of the labour force, from lathe operators, chippers, riveters and truck drivers to switchboard operators, secretaries, nurses, teachers, doctors and so on, the main issue is what to do with themselves when they are not getting paid for doing it, or learning a trade, as in school. It is obvious that no use of this time can be tolerated that will interfere with our political economy, the gross national product, or with stupidity, and that therefore there can be no education for enlightenment after hours. Fishing, boating, bowling, cabinet making, sex, and fixing up the basement can be engaged in because they help maximize the gross national product, but painting and reading not only make very minor contributions, as compared to the others, but too much reading of philosophy, history, etc., can be threatening to the system for they bring enlightenment.

People who have been through our educational system, however, will not use their leisure for anything but fun and games. It must also be borne in mind that an educational system that trains people for enlightening activities during leisure would threaten the occupational and even the class structure. If too many people, on the basis of leisure-time learning, were to start changing their occupations, considerable instability would be introduced into the occupational structure and hence into the class system. Hence there is a fundamental contradiction between the idea of productive leisure on the one hand and the maintenance of our present political economy on the other.

Vulnerability. There is no more vulnerable white-collar group than educators. For the most part without unions, subject to the whims of principals, superintendents, boards of education and local parent organizations, elementary and high-school teachers stand unprotected at the bottom of one of the most extended pyramids of power in the country. Hence they are in no position, even should they desire, to teach anything that might challenge the cultural features of which I have spoken. What I have said applies equally to so-called higher education, for there we see that educators are on the whole untroubled by problems of academic freedom, because, having come through the mill, they have divested themselves of dangerous thoughts, so that they have, on the whole, no freedom to worry about. They are self-imprisoned without knowing it. What would they teach that is unconventional? In my own discipline there are some brave men who have spoken in public against the war in Vietnam, but anthropology as an academic discipline is more innocent of dangerous thoughts than the late Pope John. What has become invulnerable also becomes rigid, because life has become safe. Thus invulnerable people are frozen, no longer because of fear alone, but because, by the miracle of the dialectic, they have come to feel so protected. Why venture out? Since invulnerability is thus a self-reinforcing system, it acts as an immovable obstacle to enlightenment.

Narrowness. Education must be narrow, it must not ask questions like 'Does life have meaning?' 'What is meaning?' 'What is the purpose of social life?' 'What is the place in life of compassion, solicitude, wisdom?' 'Is there a *world* history?' 'Is one country's richness a function of another's poverty?' 'Is my country best?'

It is clear that broadening the questions asked would also question our political economy as presently constituted. A general examination of the question of meaning in life by the whole population would immediately drive the Dow Jones index through the bottom, because people interested in the question would not play the market.

Yet it is clear that stupidity divides peoples, and it follows that the emphasis on socially acceptable intellectual sabotage is proving, right here and now, that man will be burnt to ashes in the fires of his own stupidity and ignorance. It is clear that the historic necessity of stupidity is now a historic anachronism. Stupidity has served its function but it became obsolescent, shortly after the discovery of metallurgy, for at that time the combination of stupidity and weaponry began to become so powerful that mankind itself was threatened. Combined with the black plague, the Hundred Years War almost eliminated mankind from Europe. Stupidity once served a useful function for although it separated men, it also enabled each nation and people to develop its own unique way of life, separate from penetration by the ideas of others. Narrowness and stupidity were, then, nature's own way of experimenting with a vast variety of forms. It was a kind of national stupidity that paradoxically gave us immense cultural and national creativity; so that each little island in the Pacific, each tribe in the jungle of Africa or in the forests of the New World developed its own art, music, folklore and ideology in arrogant contempt of others. It was this kind of stupidity that looked down on the culture of others; this kind of stupidity that was uncritically accepting of one's own way of life as the best and the only possible one, that in a paradoxical way was creative of the vast variety of human culture. Today this is obviously obsolete; and the fact that the whole world is now busy imitating one another in art, in music, in literature, in agriculture, science and industry is proof of the fact that primordial stupidity and narrowness is on its way out. The remaining strongholds of stupidity yet remain in political economy, social life and religion. The continued fostering of stupidity and ignorance in these areas contributes to the division of mankind, prevents nations and religions from joining the human race, and leads to wars and continued religious quarrels. It is time to understand that everything must be taught, whether it be the goodness and the evil of our own system, the goodness as well as the evils of other systems, the nature of the white power structure that continues to disfranchise the Negro, the nature of sham, and the tricks of logic that others use to deceive us.

The last topic is unity in diversity. All great movements start with a tiny group of people of passionate conviction. Typically they are ready to die for their ideals. They fight, they are tortured, they see their brothers and sisters tortured and killed and their families destroyed. They endure extreme hardships of food, weather and fear. They hide in the forests, in the hills, in holes in the ground. They fight against great odds with feeble weapons: but, inspired by their example, others join them, because, since the tiny group suffers as does the population they represent, they gain the support of the population and eventually win. There is nothing like victory, however, to convince a man that he is right; there is nothing like triumph over vast obstacles to convince a movement that they are the chosen ones, that they alone, from here, are always right and that dissent is treason. The feeling of treason stems not only from the disagreement but from the fact that disagreement itself represents a split in the monolithic structure of idea and force that carried the group to victory. There is nothing like victory forged in the heat of suffering to create a solid block of steel; there is nothing so much as a victory like that to convince a fighter that there is no such thing as disagreement but merely treason. It is the frightful stupidity of convinced victory.

Success makes men stupid and carries with it the seeds of its own dissolution. A characteristic of the stupidity of convinced victory is that it does not understand that change is inevitable. To the victorious, time and cultural variability are merely circumstances of existence to be bent to the convictions that accomplished victory. Under these circumstances the possibility of unity in diversity cannot be seen; and internal challenges merely force the original warriors to freeze more and more in their original fixed positions. The more diversity arises within their range the more they freeze and the more violent their reaction. In all great movements, however, these are transitory phases. The diversity that is becoming more and more visible in the communist countries should not be heralded joyfully as a disintegration of the enemy but rather as a happy relaxation of a group that is surer of itself and so is more willing to accept dissent. The diversity within socialism ranges from the various mixtures of capitalism and socialism in Mexico, Norway, Sweden and India, to the stricter but yet loose forms in Yugoslavia, where eighty per cent of the land is still in private hands, and the rigid, but – mind this – brand new communism of China.

All over the world mankind is moving towards unity and diversity both at the same time. For mankind the unity consists in the desire for a better life achieved through peace; the diversity consists in the recognition that the total uniformity of mankind is not yet at hand and may never be. Solid structures are splitting up as people realize and are compassionate towards each other's diversity; and diverse peoples unite as they comprehend the identity of each other's needs. To me this is the essence of human ecumenism.

In concluding I turn to the problem of the Negro among us, and I begin with a discussion of two little seven-year-olds whom I shall call David Roger and Rachel Potter. Both live in a *de facto* segregated housing development and both are poor. Rachel's father lives at home, and although, as a black man, he is able to earn an income only at the poverty line, he is a good father. The furniture in the Potters' house is modest but orderly and in condition and the house is clean. Mrs Potter stays home and takes care of the house and children. At home Rachel plays school with her little friends. The Potters are active in a religious movement, the literature of the movement is around the house, and the family has study periods devoted to it.

Though David lives in the same development, his life is very different. His house is a mess and nobody has a permanent place to sleep. Neither his mother nor father lives in the home nor with each other; but he and his three sisters are taken care of by his fifty-nine-year-old, illiterate, confused great-grandmother who has had a stroke and whose eyes are failing. The family exists almost wholly on public assistance, and the Aid for Dependent Children cheques, which are sent to the mother, are not spent on the children. Mrs Thompson, the great-grandmother, is at her wits' end, so that for the slightest thing she is apt to take a plastic covered extension cord and beat the children, though she loves them. Though David's mother does not live permanently in the home, she appears from time to time, but his father never does. The children never play school nor do homework but watch television. In the household lives James, a violent, borderline psychotic great-uncle who hits David. When David, understandably, started to disappear from home, staying out until two and three in the morning, Mrs Thompson, beside herself with fear, rounded up the father, who obliged her by beating David with a strap for an hour, and then disappeared. David has not run away since.

Surprisingly enough, David and Rachel are performing at the same level in the first grade. The reason for this, however, must be understood in order that, in an ecumenical movement directed towards the human race, we may understand the problem. David's running away from home cannot be understood unless we comprehend his school situation.

In kindergarten he had a tyrannical, irascible Negro teacher who apparently believed that the only way to make such kids mind is by hitting them, and she was free with her blows, both with hands and stick. Merely being unable to answer a question was sometimes enough for her to let fly. Since David also was hit, kindergarten merely duplicated for him the harsh home environment. There was no relief. Rachel however was quiet and was never seen to be hit. When the children got to first grade they were both in the class of Mrs Trask, a sensitive Negro woman, who worked hard with David, and at the end of the first year David and Rachel received identical report cards, even though David had got into trouble with the school authorities and been hit.

What is the significance of all of this for the unity of the human race? In the first place we see that not all ghetto families are the same, having their Potters and their Rogers; and in the second place we see that harshness with children often merely duplicates home conditions and is therefore no help to the children, but rather destroys them.

One of our most striking discoveries has been the harshness with which some Negro teachers treat their Negro children; misguided perhaps by the idea that this is the only thing they understand or by the feeling of fear that comes over them when they see these ghetto children who remind them of the source from which they themselves come. Thus we see within an oppressed group factors that contribute to the perpetuation of the condition from which they are trying to escape. It goes without saying that behind it all lies the white man's centuries of torture and degradation of the Negro: but we must remember that a tormented group, like the Negroes, may often turn its own torment against itself.

Finally we come to the issue of black power, which again throws us into the lap of disunity. Stokely Carmichael, the brilliant prophet of the movement, is disillusioned with the *friendly* relations Negroes have had with whites within the movement. In an article published in the *New York Times* of 5 August 1966, he says that Negroes can never feel at ease with the whites in the civil-rights movement because Negroes always feel inferior and because they feel that sooner or later they will somehow become captives of the very whites who are helping them. Whites, he says, must therefore be excluded from the movement though their help will be accepted from outside of it.

The disappointing thing about this declaration is its divisiveness, its turning out of friends. The fact that hundreds of whites have gone to gaol, been beaten and some even permanently damaged and killed in the interests of Negro rights is discounted. Mr Carmichael does not seem to understand that all revolts of the depressed have drawn on the education and dedication of the idealistic members of the oppressing class, for the oppressed ones, because of disfranchisement and consequent lack of education, must obtain from the oppressors the powers they need. All revolutions are sold down the river from time to time from within, but the unity of Negroes and whites that has produced the civil-rights movement has been relatively free from the outright, informing and bloody treachery of other revolutions that sent thousands to death by shooting, hanging or by starving in concentration camps. Ten years ago there was hardly a civil-rights movement at all.

I have mentioned the case of the Negro to illustrate again the point that our vulnerabilities always turn against us and fracture the unity we need as members of the human race. The brutality with which David is treated at home and in school is the actual creation of the brutality visited by white men on the Negro, yet it paradoxically turns against the Negro to maintain white brutality because it deprives Negroes of the brains and strength they need to overcome it. The movement for black power, feeling past failures acutely, turns on its friends. Thus, in black power the white man need not fear for himself but rather sorrow for the Negro.

These are problems for all of us: beset by real and phantasied vulnerabilities, we find it impossible to distinguish between friend and foe, to discern where the real enemy lies because he is often hidden, and it takes education, careful analysis and patience to tell who he is.

At home and abroad, among Negroes and whites, Christians and Jews, the enemy is always the total system within which one lives. This is what has to be examined so that we are not trapped into destroying ourselves, while we think we are destroying the enemy.

About the Author

JULES HENRY was born in New York City in 1904. He studied under Franz Boas and Ruth Benedict at Columbia University, where he received his doctorate in anthropology in 1936. Dr. Henry taught at Columbia University, the University of Chicago, and until his death in 1969, at Washington University in St. Louis.

He was a Research Associate at the Sonia Shankman Orthogenic School and was a Fellow at the Center for Advanced Study in the Behavioral Sciences at Stanford. He also served as consultant to the National Institute of Mental Health and the World Health Organization, among others, as well as a number of psychiatric hospitals. His articles have been widely published in professional and general journals. He is the author of *Doll Play of Pilagá Indian Children* (with his wife Zunia Henry), *Jungle People, Culture Against Man, Pathways to Madness* and *On Education.*

VINTAGE POLITICAL SCIENCE
AND SOCIAL CRITICISM

VINTAGE WORKS OF SCIENCE
AND PSYCHOLOGY